REMOTE SENSING AND GIS FOR NATURAL RESOURCE MANAGEMENT

Edited by

C H Power, L J Rosenberg and I Downey

The Natural Resources Institute (NRI) is a scientific institute within the University of Greenwich, and is an internationally recognized centre of expertise in research and consultancy in the environment and natural resources sector. Its principal aim is to increase the productivity of renewable natural resources in developing countries in a sustainable way by promoting development through science.

Production of this publication was funded by the United Kingdom's Overseas Development Administration.

Price £10.00

No charge is made for single copies of this publication sent to governmental and educational establishments, research institutions and non-profit-making organizations working in countries eligible for British Government Aid. Free copies cannot normally be addressed to individuals by name but only under their official titles. When ordering, please quote **LR13**.

Natural Resources Institute
ISBN 0 85954 454-0

Contents

PANEL DISCUSSION

COLOUR PLATE

POSTERS

Foreword

These proceedings contain the collective texts of papers presented at the Remote Sensing Society one day technical meeting and workshop jointly organized by the University of Greenwich School of Earth Sciences and the Environmental Science Department of the Natural Resources Institute at their Chatham Maritime site in Kent, UK, on 19 December 1995. The meeting was structured into the four main sessions (listed below) reflected in the proceedings section headings.

Natural resources management is, in essence, a wide-ranging and diverse subject. As such, the solutions to its challenges, problems and methodology necessitate the contribution of scientists and practitioners from many disciplines, particularly when the computer technologies of GIS and remote sensing are incorporated into these solutions.

The structure of the technical meeting and workshop was designed to bring together users and practitioners of remote sensing and GIS from all avenues of natural resources management, and from any geographical region (UK, Europe, developing world, or on a global perspective), to enable them to gain awareness of other activities and to discuss the issues, problems and solutions they have encountered. The meeting was inspired by the increasingly apparent global need for regular environmental status monitoring and impact assessment.

The data, techniques and methodologies provided by GIS and remote sensing are capable of greatly assisting the implementation of environmental monitoring systems. Therefore, resource managers or agencies, and practitioners of remote sensing and GIS technology (in both the developed and developing world), need to work closely together to improve and sustain their activities in support of natural resource management. Developments in the technology for earth observation and spatial information analysis have often concentrated on more expensive, high precision and spatial resolution systems and (in many cases) have overlooked more affordable effective methods and technology.

The development of appropriate, reliable methodologies is particularly relevant in the context of the growing need for regular environmental status monitoring, conservation, and environmental impact assessment. This is true for developing nations as well as for the developed, post-industrial world.

The meeting opened with welcoming messages from Mr Peter Thompson of NRI, Dr Alistair Baxter from the School of Earth Sciences, University of Greenwich, and Dr Colin Mitchell of the Remote Sensing Society, on behalf of the joint host organizations.

The addresses presented in the keynote session were designed to establish three main threads for the day. These were first, to identify both the types of activities currently using GIS and remote sensing in the developing world and the future needs of developing nations, second, to provide an insight into developed world implementation of GIS and remote sensing for natural resource management, and finally, to explore whether GIS and remote sensing can be used effectively for commercial projects in natural resource management.

Ian Haines, Head of Research in the Natural Resources Research Department at the Overseas Development Administration, outlined the current pressures on environmental and natural resource management in developing countries. By contrast, the second keynote address, given by Richard Wadsworth from the NERC Institute of Terrestrial Ecology, summarized GIS and remote sensing perspectives in the developed world and their application to natural resource planning in the UK. The final keynote presentation by Graham Deane of Huntings Technical Services Ltd addressed the critical question in the commercial context: 'are these data/(technologies) good value for money?'

These addresses were followed by a variety of oral presentations given at technical paper sessions during the morning and afternoon. The meeting concluded with more than an hour of panel discussion. A report summarizing the outcomes of the panel discussion has been included in section four of these proceedings. In addition to the four sessions, delegates and sponsors were invited to present poster papers to widen discussion during the refreshment intervals. The texts of these poster papers have been included in the final section of the proceedings. The structure of the Meeting was as follows:

Session 1:   **Keynote addresses**
- Remote Sensing and GIS: A Development Perspective
  (Ian Haines, ODA)
- The Role of Remote Sensing in a Land Use Planning Decision
    Support System
  (Richard Wadsworth, Natural Environment Research Council
    Institute of Terrestrial Ecology)
- Natural Resources Management: Commercial Perspectives
  (Graham Deane, Huntings Technical Services Ltd)

Session 2:   **Techniques and methodologies**
Remote Sensing and GIS Applied to Natural Resource Management

Session 3:   **Applications Case Studies**
Remote Sensing and GIS Applied to Natural Resource Management

Session 4:   **Panel Discussion**

The editors would like to thank the Remote Sensing Society, the Natural Resources Institute and the University of Greenwich for hosting the meeting, the Overseas Development Administration for assisting with the publication of these proceedings, and the respective companies listed in Appendix 1 for sponsoring and supporting the event.

Many grateful thanks are also due to John Couzens, the secretarial staff at the University of Greenwich School of Earth Sciences, and the student assistants who helped with the running and administration for the meeting.

Dr Clare Power (University of Greenwich)
Dr Jane Rosenberg and Mr Ian Downey (Natural Resources Institute)
Chatham Maritime, February 1996

KEYNOTE ADDRESSES

Remote Sensing and GIS: A Development Perspective

Ian Haines

Natural Resources Research Department, Overseas Development Administration, 94 Victoria Street, London, SW1E 5JL, UK.

INTRODUCTION

In this address, I am invited to give a development practitioner's perspective on the roles which remote sensing and GIS have to play in furthering the sustainable development of natural resources in the world's developing countries.

The task is not an easy one. The potential for remote sensing and GIS across a variety of applications is great, but selling the technology and more importantly, using it to its maximum effect to influence decision making, is often much more difficult. This difficulty is compounded by the fact that many remote sensing and GIS specialists have a "have technology will travel" expectation, rather than an approach which asks "what are the main problems faced by developing countries and how can remote sensing and GIS help in solving them".

Rightly or wrongly, remote sensing and GIS are commonly held to be technology driven, expensive, data hungry, information poor, highly precise and First World focused, and as such, inappropriate technologies for the needs of developing countries. To correct this false impression, how might the priorities of developing countries be identified and what guidance can development agencies give to remote sensing and GIS practioners?

THE DEVELOPING COUNTRY FOCUS

The Needs of Developing Countries

The links between poverty, population growth and environmental degradation are complex and as difficult to evaluate as the links between affluence, high patterns of consumption and rising environmental standards. With increasing urbanization, population growth and economic diversification, environmental and natural resource management has become a key issue in the developing world. These concerns focus not only on efficient resource utilization for sustainable economic development, but also on the conservation of biodiversity (at genetic, whole organism and habitat level) and the maintenance of vital biospheric processes in land, aquatic and 'interface' systems such as coastal ecosystems. In many developing countries, these issues have led to a growing realization that effective environment and natural resource management requires reliable and timely information, and to an increasing awareness of the need to develop an integrated approach for improving our capacity to manage natural resources on a more rational basis. Remote sensing and GIS are often integral parts of this capacity building process.

In addition to national development plans, development priorities and needs from a global perspective are well presented in Agenda 21, the Plan of Action for the 21st century agreed at the United Nations Conference on Environment and Development. Some aspects might lend themselves to remote sensing and GIS inputs.

- Combatting desertification

- Promoting sustainable human settlement development

- Integrating environment and development in decision making

- Protection of the atmosphere

- Integrated approach to the planning and management of land resources

- Combatting deforestation

- Managing fragile ecosystems

- Promoting sustainable agriculture and rural development

- Conservation of biological diversity

- Protection of the oceans and coastal areas

- Protection of freshwater resources

- Transfer of environmentally sound technology, co-operation and capacity building

- Science for sustainable development

- Information for decision makers

Figure 1. Some Agenda 21 chapters and programme areas

The Role of the Development Agencies

As a development agency, the ODA needs to relate its activities to its overall purpose of improving the lot of the poorest people in developing countries. Our business is poverty reduction, strengthening economies and promoting human development. Enhancing productive capacity and helping developing countries tackle environmental problems are important components of our work.

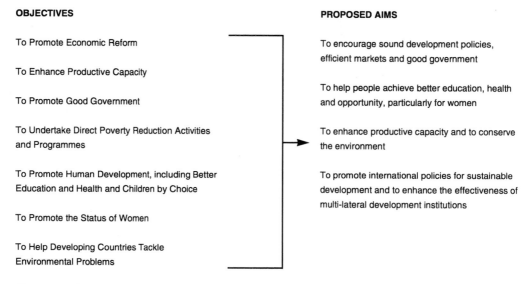

OBJECTIVES

To Promote Economic Reform

To Enhance Productive Capacity

To Promote Good Government

To Undertake Direct Poverty Reduction Activities and Programmes

To Promote Human Development, including Better Education and Health and Children by Choice

To Promote the Status of Women

To Help Developing Countries Tackle Environmental Problems

PROPOSED AIMS

To encourage sound development policies, efficient markets and good government

To help people achieve better education, health and opportunity, particularly for women

To enhance productive capacity and to conserve the environment

To promote international policies for sustainable development and to enhance the effectiveness of multi-lateral development institutions

Figure 2. ODA departmental aims and objectives

When looking at the role of remote sensing and GIS in development, we have to consider what these tools can offer to the management of renewable and non-renewable natural resources, and what contribution they can make to meeting the ODA's aims. The real challenge is to make remote sensing and GIS technology affordable, useful and accessible.

Development agencies need answers to four fundamental questions when evaluating the role of this technology in sustainable development programmes:

- is there a problem to be solved through the application of the technology?

- is the technology affordable and relevant?

- are the results likely to be reliable, meaningful and interpretable?

- will the results have influence, i.e., how can the data be translated into information which will influence decision makers?

If technology application and technology co-operation are parts of development activity, we need to ensure that the institutional requirements (including trained personnel), longer-term financing, and local commitment to apply the technology, are in place.

Increasingly, community level consultation and validation of results are the approaches taken by ODA. Applications of remote sensing and GIS need to be related to the needs of intended beneficiaries. They should therefore be developed in close consultation with intended users, i.e., institutions in developing countries need a stake in the development and application of the technology.

For some time, the ODA has been supporting programmes in developing countries in which remote sensing and GIS are integral parts of the problem solving activities. In view of the venue for this meeting, it is highly appropriate that I should mention that at the forefront of these programmes is the NRI-led local application of remote sensing techniques (LARST) (see figures 3 and 4). These low-cost, in-country systems are designed to provide environmental information directly to decision makers.

For environmental monitoring purposes, the LARST approach has the advantages of being focused, flexible, on-the-spot, and with a relatively quick

- Vegetation Monitoring

- Wildlife Park Management/Animal Tracking

- Pest Habitat Monitoring

- Weather Forecasting

- Rainfall Estimation

- Early Warning Systems Support

- Information Dissemination

> Other applications might include: resource assessment; crop production modelling; rangeland management; fire risk assessment; biodiversity and habitat maintenance; river catchment management; forest margin management; peri-urban environment management; monitoring extractive industries; monitoring land degradation.

Figure 3. Typical LARST applications

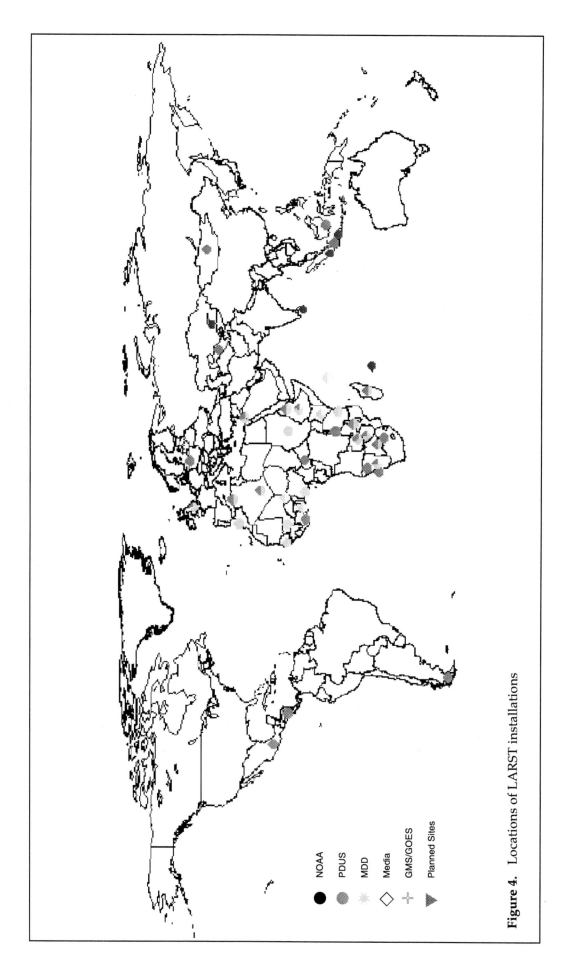

Figure 4. Locations of LARST installations

turn-round time. The principal advantage is the ability to collect and disseminate real time information, but as with all technologies, applications need to be 'sold' in terms of the development constraints which need to be addressed, the appropriateness of the technology proposed, its utility, and its affordability.

CONCLUSIONS

Uninformed decisions and subsequent responses are likely to result in misdirected effort and significant costs. Monitoring environmental factors, even on a limited scale, can help to confirm or deny issues before they become unmanageable. Analysis need not be complex or exhaustive, but it should be sufficient to demonstrate the issues clearly, to both the public and the decision makers, in order to enable rational decisions to be taken.

Remote sensing and GIS are extremely powerful tools but in spite of their capabilities there are still constraints to their effective application. These are due to lack of co-operation between the data suppliers and the users, lack of in-country expertise, inadequate institutional linkages, poor data quality, and a lack of commitment in many developing countries to establish clearly defined priorities. As ever increasing volumes of data are collected by various national, regional and international agencies, the integration of information becomes increasingly important. Unfortunately, few give sufficient attention to integration, so the gap between data producers and information users increases.

The challenge for remote sensing and GIS is to produce results that are reliable, understandable and persuasive enough to influence the decision making process. If these criteria are not met, remote sensing and GIS as tools for sustainable development are unlikely to become best sellers in developing countries.

The Role of Remote Sensing in a Land Use Planning Decision Support System

Richard Wadsworth

Environmental Information Centre, Institute of Terrestrial Ecology, Abbots Ripton, Huntingdon, Cambs, PE17 2LS, UK.

ABSTRACT

The use of remotely sensed data for natural resource planning in the UK is illustrated by reference to the NERC-ESRC Land Use Programme (NELUP). NELUP provided for the integrated analysis of the forces driving and opposing land use change in a river catchment (initially the River Tyne, later the River Cam). Within NELUP, the emphasis has been on allowing decision makers and other land use planners to make better or more informed decisions about the causes and consequences of land use change. The Decision Support System developed by NELUP uses the concept of land cover to allow the hydrological, economic and ecological impacts of change to be transferred between different parts of the system. Remotely sensed land cover data ultimately provided the most useful estimates of land cover in the UK. Models of hydrology, ecology and economics operate on a variety of spatial and temporal scales. The models are nested to allow the choice of the most appropriate scheme for the 'scale' of the problem being addressed. Remotely sensed estimates of land cover provide input to most of these models, and enables the refinement of the distribution of more spatially aggregated data sets.

INTRODUCTION AND BACKGROUND TO NELUP

The importance of remotely sensed data in natural resource planning can be illustrated by discussing the role of remote sensing in the NERC-ESRC Land Use Programme (NELUP). Within NELUP, remotely sensed data were used by economists, ecologists and hydrologists striving to understand and communicate the interlinked factors shaping land use within a river catchment. Remotely sensed data were used by these diverse disciplines in a variety of ways: as a description of the environment; as input to models; and for model validation.

The Bruntland Report (WCED, 1987) argued that economic growth and environmental conservation were not simple opposites and that economic development strategies could be chosen which would sustain the environmental capacities and relations needed for the future. The issue of an integrated approach to the management of land and water was emphasized by the Earth Summit in Rio (UNDC, 1993) and by the subsequent strategy and programmes outlined by the British Government (HM Government, 1994a, 1994b). For harmony to exist between economic change and the environment, there must be broad agreement between the large number of actors involved in land and natural resource use. The proposal for funding NELUP presented to the Research Councils in 1988 includes the following key section:

> "to investigate techniques for producing a Decision Support System (DSS) for land use planning comprising the socio-economic mechanisms of land allocation constrained by our scientific understanding of the physical and ecological environments. The synthesis of understanding is to be achieved mainly through the use of modelling approaches which will form the basis of a Decision Support System."

When trying to build a generalized systems framework of land use within a catchment, a number of abstractions and simplifications are required; data compilation leads to the incorporation of biophysical and economic modelling into the DSS which presents information to social organizations. Within this framework, reliance on published national data sets rather than on a specific data collection exercise is a key part of the NELUP philosophy. A more detailed discussion of how and why NELUP was set up can be found in O'Callaghan (1995).

The prototype DSS was constructed for the River Tyne. A catchment provides a compromise between the individual entrepreneur and the national scale at which policies are formulated. Within the 3000 km^2 of the Tyne catchment, land use varies from forestry, water-gathering and semi-natural moor, through more intensive livestock and arable agriculture, to industrial areas; elevations vary from over 800 m to sea level. Twenty-three of the 25 land covers defined in the ITE land cover map, and 19 of the 32 ITE land classes, are present. The methodology and framework have been verified by extending the DSS to cover the predominantly lowland, arable and environmentally stressed River Cam catchment.

BASIC STRUCTURE OF NELUP

NELUP has used the concept of land cover as a way of unifying and communicating information between the different parts of the project. Land cover is manipulated to achieve economic objectives (growing crops or trees, harvesting water, being covered in concrete and so on); it also intercepts precipitation (which runs off, is absorbed, is transpired or evaporated) and is critical to the hydrological cycle, and it strongly influences which plants and animals are present. Within each main area of the study (economics, ecology, hydrology), a hierarchy of models has been developed to describe phenomena at different spatial and temporal scales. Data and models are accessed through a Graphical User Interface (GUI) designed to encourage users to think about the information rather than the mechanics of obtaining it. The GUI is fast, efficient and effective. A full description of the DSS may be found in McClean et al. (1995) and the basic layout of the GUI can be seen in Figure 1.

AGRICULTURAL ECONOMICS

The economics component occupies a key position in the operations of NELUP. In terms of area, agricultural operations are the most important land use operations carried out over the catchment. It is thought that over short to medium time scales, many land use changes are driven by responses to the economic climate. Economic models exist at the catchment scale and the individual farm scale. The objective of the catchment economics model is to forecast, in a quantitative way, patterns of agricultural and forestry land and associated resources use under different policy scenarios (Moxey et al., 1995). The farm level models were developed under JAEP (Joint Agriculture and Environment Programme). They illustrate how individual farmers, constrained by a particular set of resources (land, labour, capital, livestock, machinery) can respond to changes in these physical resources and financial incentives (Oglethorpe and O'Callaghan, 1995).

Although many motives other than profit maximization exist, farmers can be seen to respond over relatively short time periods to changes in product prices and incentives from subsidies. Such responses were graphically illustrated by the uptake of oilseed rape in the 1980s and more recently, by the uptake of linseed. A large (2740 x 1349) linear programme of the entire catchment has been constructed and validated against agricultural census data. The catchment is divided into agricultural capability classes following the methodology developed by MLURI (Bibby et al., 1991). Each enterprise exists at a number of distinctly different intensities, and the land capability class defines, for each enterprise, the expected output given a particular vector of inputs. The physical input-output relationships are derived using a crop model EPIC (Erosion Productivity Impact Calculator); financial input-output relationships are derived from the Farm Business Survey and the distribution of agricultural resources, from the MAFF June census. The model is run on pairs of years so that the optimal output from one year becomes the initial conditions for the next year. Rates of change between years are constrained by physical and financial factors.

Within the economics component of NELUP, remotely sensed data are used to verify the distribution of land use types. It should be noted that ITE's land cover map does not distinguish agricultural use, so a single arable class exists; managed grassland also covers a variety of activities. It does, however, provide confirmation of the general land cover patterns and allows the exclusion of non-agricultural land.

HYDROLOGY

The primary goal of hydrological models within NELUP is to simulate the patterns of water and nitrate movement in a catchment (Adams et al., 1995). As land cover changes, evapotranspiration and run-off alter, and this affects the flow of water and the transport of nitrates. NELUP contains a catchment-wide economics model. Therefore, it is possible to estimate changes in farm inputs, such as artificial fertilizers, as well as changes in land cover. Two hydrological models exist within NELUP: SHETRAN and ARNO. Although the models perform the same task, they differ considerably in the spatial resolution at which they operate and in how computer intensive they are to process. In most cases, the ARNO model would probably be used to 'screen' a new scenario and assess where and how the more detailed SHETRAN should be used.

The ARNO model uses a lumped soil moisture accounting modelling approach. The catchment is divided into a number of sub-basins. Each sub-basin is described by solving a soil moisture balance accounting model and explicitly routing surface, inter-zone and groundwater flow. Aggregate sub-basin output can be routed into the primary river network, but spatially disaggregate estimates of soil moisture, soil water content and overland flow are only available in SHETRAN. SHETRAN is an extended version of the Système Hydrologique Européen (SHE), a linked hydrological/hydraulic catchment modelling system which is physically based and spatially distributed. Within the Tyne, SHETRAN operates at a resolution of 1 km.

The hydrological models use the ITE land cover map to provide estimates of the distribution of hydrologically distinct land covers. The potential exists for using remotely sensed data to estimate hydrological parameters, such as actual transpiration rates, which are related to land cover, but it has not yet been tried.

ECOLOGY

Ecological modelling within NELUP has two aims: to predict the occurrence of species; and to predict how the distribution will change in response to changes in land cover (Rushton et al., 1995). Within a catchment, there are so many species, so many habitats and so many potential changes, that process-based models can only cover a tiny fraction of the alternatives. An associative matrix model is used for plants and invertebrates where only broad associations may be consistently inferred between the observed presence of the organism and the environment, and where the individual organism can complete its life cycle in a single habitat unit. A model of this type has the distinct advantage that the change in distribution of all plant species found in the Tyne, and selected groups of invertebrates, can be estimated for any change in land cover. A second associative model relies on the environmental data contained in the National Vegetation Survey. By using multivariate statistics (ordination and detrended correspondence analysis), it is possible to relate individual communities to a suite of environmental and management practices. When management practices change, new ordination scores can be generated and a trajectory of change estimated. For organisms which rely on a suite of habitats and for which the data exists, habitat preference may be estimated using Baysian statistics. A Baysian approach is currently implemented for selected bird species, but it could be extended to other 'landscape-dependent' species for which published data exist.

For the associative model, remotely sensed land cover data are used as the major determinants for the location of plants and animals within the catchment. For 'Baysian' species, analogues between habitat preference and remotely sensed land cover have to be determined.

EXAMPLES OF THE USE OF REMOTELY SENSED DATA IN THE DSS

Within NELUP, the emphasis was on ways of supporting decisions about land use and because of this, the system was designed to be used in a number of ways. At its simplest, the DSS provides access to an extensive database. Such a resource can be used for National Rivers Authority (NRA) catchment plans, landscape assessments such as those recommended by the Countryside Commission (1993), or other overviews and audits. It can be used to perform simple analysis, search, and comparison operations on the data. At its most complex, the models can be used in reactive or proactive analysis of policies. For example, a user interested in changing the livestock subsidy on upland sheep can investigate the economic impact on a range of 'typical' farms and on the catchment as a whole. Changing livestock numbers (and use of agricultural inputs) will affect the land cover and therefore, the quantity and quality of water in the rivers and the distribution of plants and animals. The user can decide whether the predicted changes are acceptable. A case for using the NELUP system for Environmental Impact Assessment (EIA) is made by Wadsworth (1995), and the use of NELUP in Strategic Land Use Planning by Haslam and Newson (1995). Use of remotely sensed and other environmental data will be illustrated by two examples.

Example 1 Contingency Analysis
Figure 1 demonstrates the simplest use of the DSS to compare the distribution of two variables. Window 1 (top left) shows the proportion of each 1 km square dominated by peat soils and window 2 (top right) shows the distribution of 'bog' as defined by remote sensing. Window 3 (bottom right) shows the two distributions multiplied together to emphasize the areas in common (note that the user needs to be aware that the result is in 'undefined' units). The final window (bottom left) shows the contingency analysis following the binning of the data.

Example 2 Identification of Species-Rich Grassland
Hay meadows are species-rich grasslands of conservation interest; they are relatively common in the north Pennines Dales but are much less common in the Tyne. According to Rodwell (1991, 1992), traditional management involves winter grazing and a summer hay crop on moist, but not waterlogged, brown soils. Where traditional management coincides with a relatively harsh climate, species-rich swards may develop. Managed grassland as identified in the

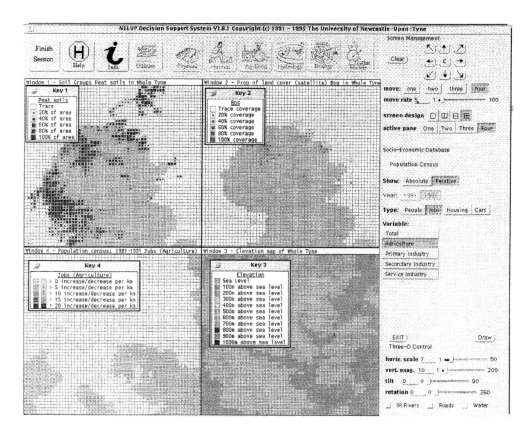

Figure 1. Example of contingency analysis, see text for details (original in colour)

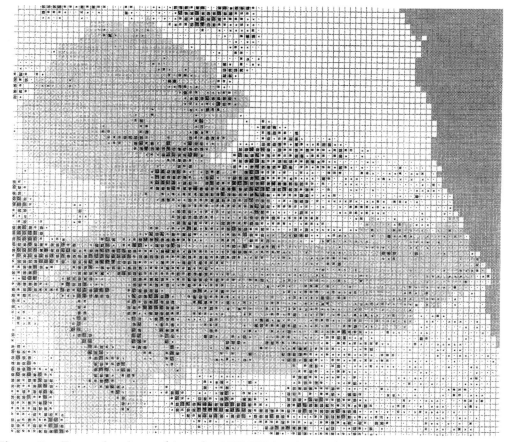

Figure 2a. Example of searching the NELUP land use database, see text for details (original in colour)

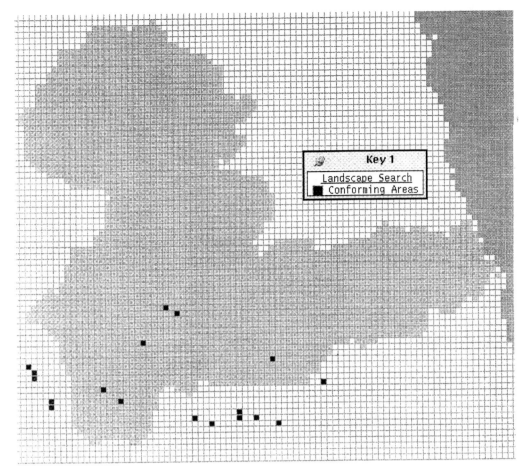

Figure 2b.

remotely sensed land cover map is very extensive in the Tyne catchment, and Wadsworth and O'Callaghan (1995) showed how the search may be narrowed considerably. Figure 2a shows the distribution of ITE land class 7 (managed grassland). Using the GUI, the following search attributes and values may be included:

land cover 'managed grassland' greater than 25% of the square
and elevation above 200 m
and gradient between 5 and 15°
and MLURI land capability 5 or worse
and south facing.

The search results in the distribution shown in Figure 2b. The identified squares are in locations identified by the *Flora of Northumberland* (Swan, 1993) as areas where hay meadows may exist.

CONCLUSIONS

The great contribution that NELUP has made to land use planning and resource management in the UK is to show that it is perfectly feasible to link together the natural and social factors influencing land use change with quantitative estimates of their effects. The system is flexible in the way it can be used and in the sorts of problems which can be tackled. Although there can be no substitute for specific detailed studies, the DSS does provide a way of screening many potential changes in a quick and efficient manner. A framework has been constructed within which data and models from economists, hydrologists and ecologists can be made accessible to non-specialists.

In the context of this paper, the importance of remotely sensed data to NELUP when endeavouring to help decision makers in England make better and more informed decisions about the factors influencing land and natural resource use has been emphasized. Remotely sensed data have been used in different ways, particularly for describing the environment, providing input to predictive models, and verifying predictions. Remotely sensed data should be seen as tools in larger projects rather than as end products.

ACKNOWLEDGEMENTS

The author would like to thank CLUWRR and in particular, Chris Mulcahy, for the reproduction of the DSS figures given in this paper. For more recent information contact:
Rae Mackay
Centre for Land Use and Water Resources Research
The University
Newcastle upon Tyne NE1 7RU

Tel. +44 191 222 6563
Fax. +44 191 222 6563
email CLUWRR@ncl.ac.uk
URL http://www.cluwrr.ncl.ac.uk

NELUP was funded by the Natural Environment Research Council and the Economic and Social Research Council.

REFERENCES

Adams, R., Dunn, S.M., Lunn, R., Mackay, R and O'Callaghan, J.R. (1995) Assessing the performance of the NELUP hydrological models for river basin planning. *Journal of Environmental Planning and Management*, **38**: 53-76.

Bibby, J.S., Douglas, H.A., Thomasson, A.J. and Robertson, J.S. (1991) *Land Capability Classification for Agriculture*. Aberdeen: Macaulay Land Use Research Institute.

Countryside Commission (1993) *Landscape Assessment Guidance*. Walgrave, Northampton.

Haslam, M. and Newson, M. (1995) The potential role for NELUP in strategic land use planning. *Journal of Environmental Planning and Management*, **38**: 137-141.

HM Government (1994a) *Sustainable Development: the UK Strategy Cm 2426*. London: HMSO.

HM Government (1994b) *Biodiversity: the UK Action Plan Cm 2428*. London: HMSO.

McClean, C.J., Watson, P.M., Wadsworth, R.A., Blaiklock, J. and O'Callaghan, J.R. (1995) Land use planning: a Decision Support System. *Journal of Environmental Planning and Management*, **38**: 77-92.

Moxey, A.P., White B. and O'Callaghan, J.R. (1995) The economic component of NELUP. *Journal of Environmental Planning and Management*, **38**: 21-34.

O'Callaghan, J.R. (1995) NELUP: an introduction. *Journal of Environmental Planning and Management*, **38**: 5-20.

Oglethorpe, D.R. and O'Callaghan, J.R. (1995) Farm-level economic modelling within a river catchment Decision Support System. *Journal of Environmental Planning and Management*, **38**: 93-106.

Rodwell, J.S. (1991) *British Plant Communities, Mires and Heaths*. Cambridge: Cambridge University Press.

Rodwell, J.S. (1992) *British Plant Communities, Grasslands and Montane Communities*. Cambridge: Cambridge University Press.

Rushton, S.P., Cherril, A.J., Tucker, K. and O'Callaghan, J.R. (1995) The ecological modelling system of NELUP. *Journal of Environmental Planning and Management*, **38**: 35-52.

Swan, G.A. (1993) *The Flora of Northumberland*. Newcastle upon Tyne: Natural History Society of Northumbria.

United Nations Development Commission (UNDC) (1993) *Agenda 21: Action Plan for the Next Century*. New York: UNDC.

Wadsworth, R.A. (1995) *Integration of Environmental Impact Assessment With Land Use Planning in a Decision Support System*. PhD thesis [unpublished]. Newcastle University, Newcastle upon Tyne.

Wadsworth, R.A. and O'Callaghan, J.R. (1995) Empirical searches of the NELUP land use database. *Journal of Environmental Planning and Management*, **38**: 107-116.

World Commission on Environment and Development (WCED) (1987) *Our Common Future*. Oxford: Oxford University Press.

Remote Sensing and GIS for Natural Resources Management: Commercial Perspectives

Graham Deane

Hunting Technical Services Limited, Thamesfield House, Boundary Way, Hemel Hempstead, Herts HP2 7SR, UK.

ABSTRACT

The management of natural resources requires access to reliable data and, more importantly, reliable and accurate information derived from these data. Where the resources manager has to pay for data and information, the immediate question arises, "are these data good value for money?". The commercial service provider has to demonstrate both the accuracy and the cost effectiveness of the products and services offered to clients; only then can a service be classed as operational.

The resources manager usually has a good idea of the quality of information that can be derived from aerial photography and, for a given specification of air-photo acquisition, expects that a predictable level of resource information can be produced. Similar predictability in the use of satellite remote sensing has now been achieved in some sectors; agricultural monitoring in Europe is now an operational activity because the customers have been convinced that the technology gives satisfactory information more cheaply than alternative approaches. Convincing the customers has required a major co-ordinated research effort. Other applications, such as providing the forester with predicted timber volumes, have not yet been developed as operational activities.

Where applications are well proven, such as land use and vegetation mapping and monitoring, the main limitations to providing resource information are data availability and the basic cost of data. A proven technology cannot help if the data are just not available or are too expensive to be afforded by the resource managers. There is a lack of satellite data covering East Africa, primarily because there are no direct data reception facilities currently in place. Recent attempts to rectify this, using a commercial approach, have failed, at least in part, because the expectations of data sales far exceeded the reality. The conclusion to be drawn is that whilst remote sensing and GIS technology could be used to prepare detailed maps (that are updated regularly to provide the monitoring function) using high resolution imagery, the financial resources to undertake such work are just not available. Much cheaper approaches have to be developed and implemented.

The minerals and hydrocarbons industry can approach natural resources mapping and management knowing that successful exploration activities can bring considerable returns on investment. Such returns can ultimately pay for complex airborne and satellite surveys; in contrast a vegetation survey is unlikely to bring any significant financial return to the resource manager commissioning the survey. An alternative approach to survey design must, therefore, be adopted, supported by appropriate scientific research.

The use of remote sensing and GIS technologies, once the techniques have been carefully developed through scientific research, is dependent upon just how much the resource manager needs the information and how well he can persuade someone to pay for it. In many earth resources studies the financial resources are insufficient for the level of detail required by the resource managers. Industry and the scientific community have to work together to find the most cost effective solution.

TECHNICAL
APPLICATIONS

Integrating Satellite Imagery and GIS: The Experience of a BNSC Funded Project to Monitor Environmentally Sensitive Areas

Robert Brown[1], Jacqueline Slater[2] and David Askew[3]

[1]Remote Sensing Applications Consultants, Mansfield Park, Medstead, Alton, Hants, GU34 5PZ, UK.

[2]ADAS, Brooklands Avenue, Cambridge, CB2 2BL, UK.

[3]ADAS, Lawnswood, Otley Road, Leeds LS16 5PY, UK.

ABSTRACT

This project assessed the suitability of satellite imagery for monitoring Environmentally Sensitive Areas (ESAs) in England, an example of agri-environment policy for the protection of landscapes and wildlife in agricultural areas. An overall objective was to encourage GIS users to use satellite imagery in land cover applications by resolving some of the technical issues constraining its integration with GIS. Satellite imagery is seen as a low-cost, large area digital data source with a historical archive which could be used more effectively in environmental monitoring. An initial review to select a proprietary system highlighted the difficulty of using a low-cost, PC-based system for this task. Land cover map updating techniques were developed which allowed baseline land cover maps, produced from air photography, to be digitally updated on-screen using satellite imagery. Application of the techniques focused on map updating, change detection, and botanical monitoring. The main study areas were The Broads and Pennine Dales ESAs. Changes from arable to grassland as a result of ESA policy were detected and mapped, using both optical and radar satellite imagery, and compared to the changes detected with air photography. The use of satellite imagery for discriminating grassland types was investigated.

INTRODUCTION

Images from satellites have often been promoted as sources of information for producing land cover maps, particularly for use within geographic information systems (GIS). However, a range of practical difficulties is encountered when implementing an operational system using this approach. These include the integration of satellite imagery (raster data) and existing land cover maps (generally vector data), limited spatial resolution of satellite data, availability and timing of imagery, and inadequacy of automatic classification techniques. Increasingly, mapping is carried out digitally and the information is analysed within a GIS. Satellite imagery offers particular advantages when used in conjunction with GIS but to be effective, it must be fully integrated into GIS.

In the context of land cover or land use mapping, the potential benefit of satellite imagery is the availability of large area coverage as seamless data at a relatively low cost. Imagery is available over a long time span and has been supplied in digital form for many years. It represents one of the few sources of raw data for producing land cover maps which can be easily incorporated into many GIS.

In 1993, Remote Sensing Applications Consultants (RSAC) in collaboration with ADAS were awarded a contract by the British National Space Centre (BNSC) to develop a land cover map updating system using satellite imagery. With technical support from Earth Observation Sciences Limited, the project has been built around a specific practical requirement to test the suitability and accuracy of satellite imagery for monitoring an agri-environment scheme, the Environmentally Sensitive Areas (ESAs). The overall objective of the project was to reduce some of the technical barriers which have constrained the use of satellite data for mapping land cover. This was achieved by creating a land cover map updating system which featured user-friendly utilities. The project concentrated on protected landscapes which are subject to increasing pressure, especially from the intensification of agriculture.

ENVIRONMENTALLY SENSITIVE AREAS

ESAs are areas designated throughout the UK where the landscape, wildlife or historic interest are of national importance and need protection from the changes brought about by the development of more intensive farming methods. Within

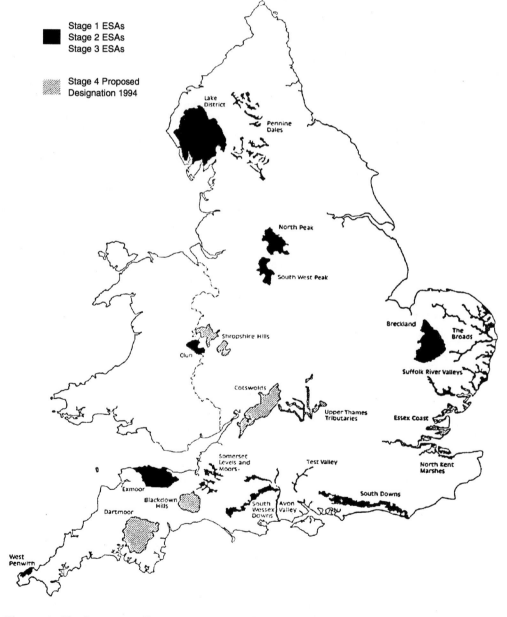

Figure 1. Environmentally sensitive areas in England

ESAs, farmers who join the scheme are offered payments for managing their land in such a way as to preserve or enhance the desired environmental features. The locations of ESAs in England are shown in Figure 1.

Environmental monitoring of the impact of the ESA scheme in England has been carried out by ADAS on behalf of the Ministry of Agriculture, Fisheries and Food (MAFF). Previously, ADAS had relied on a combination of ground and aerial survey to conduct ESA monitoring, but they recognized the potential for complementing these sources of information with satellite imagery and digital mapping and analysis techniques. The requirements are similar to those of other organizations involved in monitoring and mapping land cover, such as national and local government authorities, National Parks and conservation organizations.

The main project objectives were to select and customize a proprietary image processing or GIS, and to test the suitability and efficiency of satellite imagery for ESA monitoring as an alternative or adjunct to existing methods. This paper concentrates on change detection, particularly between arable land and grassland, and botanical monitoring.

SYSTEMS REVIEW

Various potentially suitable image processing systems and GIS were reviewed at the end of 1993 with the hope of selecting a low-cost system based on a PC. The main requirements were to provide image processing capability with good display, the ability to import and manipulate vector land maps and raster satellite data in a common geographic reference frame, the ability to perform spatial analysis such as change detection and feature selection, on-screen digitizing over satellite imagery, high quality map output and statistics; the potential for customization to meet the needs of individual users was also required. These criteria had to be met at reasonable cost! Surprisingly, none of the PC systems available at the time fulfilled all the requirements, particularly in terms of customization and the handling of sufficient quantities of data. Nevertheless, systems are continually evolving and PC systems able to meet these requirements are expected to be available soon.

Falling hardware and software costs allowed the consideration of more sophisticated systems, with the result that a UNIX workstation-based system was selected. ERDAS IMAGINE with the VECTOR module based on ARC/INFO has been used for this project. This is a raster-based image processing system with full features for the processing of satellite imagery, full vector digital mapping capability, and GIS analysis in raster form.

DEVELOPMENT OF TECHNIQUES AND CUSTOMIZATION OF SOFTWARE

Data Preparation

Data preparation of both satellite imagery and digital maps is a necessary prerequisite for their integrated interpretation in a map updating system using a common geographic frame of reference. All imagery has been geometrically corrected and georeferenced to Ordnance Survey maps. Conversion of vector data between the existing PC-based digital mapping system (MAPDATA) format and the ARC/INFO format required a considerable amount of work. In particular, problems arose in transforming data created in a relatively simple package with a high level of error tolerance, to ARC/INFO format which demands a higher degree of data integrity. Vector data which are perfectly adequate for producing land cover maps may require significant cleaning before they can be used as a GIS layer.

Customization of the Interface

The customizing of the interface to present windows and menus in a user-specific manner proved to be less important than a full understanding of the processes available and the parameters required to use them in the desired manner. This undoubtedly depends on the particular software used, and recognizes the sophistication of the standard IMAGINE interface. Development concentrated on the creation of 'bolt-on' processes written for this project, and devising procedures required for major user needs from the available features.

Visual Map Updating

Visual map updating is an example of procedure development which could be adapted to other systems. The principles involved are the same as those for interpreting air photography, except that stereoscopic viewing is not possible. The advantage is that with on-screen digitizing, the digital map can be created directly, cutting out intermediate digitizing or scanning, and the whole project area can be viewed and interpreted seamlessly. The updating, with a 1990 satellite image, of a 1987 map created from air photo interpretation and ground survey, is described below.

A reference window was created with the 1990 image overlaid by a mask to hide non-ESA areas. The 1987 land cover map vectors were overlaid. A digital topographic map or image classification could also be used for reference.

An editing window was then created containing the 1990 image and a copy of the 1987 land cover map which formed the basis for producing the 1990 map. The reference window was used to show the area systematically, by mapsheet for example, while the editing window was used to zoom in on areas which needed changing.

Visual interpretation involved comparing existing vectors with the new satellite image, and checking for obvious boundary changes. In the case of ERDAS IMAGINE, a display masking technique aided interpretation. Areas of a particular land cover type from the 1987 map, for example arable, could be viewed by masking out all non-arable land with a uniform colour. By looking between the masked areas to the 1990 image, any changes to non-arable land could be identified. This procedure could be applied in reverse to identify changes to arable from other classes.

The 1990 map was then edited in the edit viewer. Land cover codes were altered as necessary in the map's attribute table, and changed boundaries were edited on screen over the image backdrop. The new map was then processed and checked to produce a digital version.

Change Mapping

A customized routine has been written to produce a change map from the original and updated maps. This compares two raster thematic images of land cover classes, creates an output image with a new category corresponding to each class of change (such as arable-to-grass or grass-to-arable), and tabulates the changes and measurements of the areas involved. Using the display facilities of the system, each change category, or group of categories, can be highlighted over the image as desired. A hard copy map displaying the features required can then be produced using the map composition module of the system.

Parcel Statistics

A customized routine for producing parcel statistics has also been written. This involves the calculation of mean and standard deviation values for each parcel or mapping unit of the land cover map for each of the image wavebands. A mean image can be produced consisting of a mean value for each parcel. The table can be used for analysis of relationships between image pixel values and other data sources, such as land cover classes or botanical data. The mean image can be used in multi-spectral classification if there are field boundaries. This feature has been used in the botanical monitoring work described below to extend ground survey data.

LAND COVER CHANGE DETECTION AND MAP UPDATING

The Broads ESA covers approximately 36 000 ha of river valley, marsh and fen in Norfolk and south Suffolk. Major objectives of this lowland ESA are to maintain traditional livestock farming on permanent grassland, and to extend the areas covered by traditional grazing marshes and wet meadow by arable reversion. The techniques of visual map updating, and production of change maps, have been investigated in this ESA. The main issue for land cover change mapping is to identify changes between arable and grassland.

As part of the monitoring programme for The Broads ESA, a baseline land cover map was made in 1987 from air photos at 1:10 000 scale. Air photos were re-flown in 1990 with the aim of producing land cover change data. These change data were used to assess the feasibility of satellite imagery for map updating.

On the Landsat TM imagery, grassland and arable could be consistently distinguished. Using an April 1990 image, an updated 1990 land cover map was produced using a sample area of approximately one third of the ESA. Using air photography, permanent grassland could be distinguished from recently sown, temporary grassland which is really part of an arable rotation. This temporary grassland could not be distinguished on the imagery. Therefore, all grass was initially labelled as permanent grassland, significantly over-estimating its area. Areas of change within the ESA scheme were taken as a permanent change to grassland. For the remaining areas of new grassland, fields which were in predominantly arable areas were rejected, thus reducing the over-estimation.

An accuracy assessment revealed that visual interpretation of satellite imagery still significantly over-estimated the amount of new grassland. Some areas of change were not detected. Most of the changes which were missed were either in small fields or were due to interpreter error. Some of the changes to grass outside the scheme would need to be checked in the field.

Both visual interpretations, from air photography and satellite imagery, showed that in the sample area, approximately 10% of the arable area of 1987 had reverted to grassland by 1990. The larger area of grassland from image interpretation is, as explained above, mainly due to the incorrect interpretation of arable leys as new permanent grassland. This over-estimation is offset by missing some changes to grassland in smaller fields. The estimate for new grassland in fields which are part of the ESA scheme is close, and it is assumed that changes to grassland within the scheme would be permanent. The over-estimation comes mainly from fields which not part of the scheme.

Errors of omission (changes that were missed by visual interpretation) have not been a particular problem. However, errors of commission, i.e., over-estimating the number of changes, have been. The problem has been largely due to the difficulty of discriminating grass leys from permanent grassland. Although the comparisons have assumed that the air photo interpretation is correct, it should be recognized that errors may occur with established grass leys more than 2 years old. A time series of imagery was obtained to identify land in arable rotation over a longer time period, and this is investigated below. The work has been described in more detail by Slater and Askew (1995).

Radar Satellite Imagery for Change Detection

Cloud cover is one of the major limitations when planning the regular use of optical imagery in the UK. Synthetic Aperture Radar (SAR) can acquire imagery day or night, regardless of cloud cover. SAR sensors are now becoming available on satellite platforms; the European ERS-1 and ERS-2 satellites, and the Canadian RADARSAT, are all operational. Therefore, SAR imagery can now be obtained for operational programmes in the same way as optical imagery such as LANDSAT and SPOT. However, the radar backscatter of many land cover types is poorly understood. For visual interpretation, radar images are generally viewed as multi-temporal colour composites combining three dates of acquisition. Bright colours then represent areas of change. The study assessed the value of the imagery for a practical task.

A multi-temporal composite for 1992 revealed late autumn (November) to be the best time of year for arable/grassland discrimination in this area. Images from 1991, 1992 and 1993 were visually analysed both individually and as a colour combination. Arable land could generally be discriminated from grass based on the grey tone of a single image, although there were fields where tones were ambiguous. This effect increased as fields got smaller and comprised only a few pixels.

The major use of this imagery in the context of ESA monitoring is expected to be change detection between arable and grassland, and the multi-year image has been used operationally for this in the 1995 re-survey of The Broads. The single-band radar acquisition is significantly cheaper, and its acquisition more reliable, than optical images.

Time Series for Discrimination of Permanent and Ley Grassland

Imagery was available for 1987 (TM), 1990 (TM), 1991 (ERS-1), 1992 (ERS-1), 1993 (ERS-1) and 1994 (TM). The 1990 imagery had already been interpreted, so the 1991–1994 images were used to check 22 parcels where there were discrepancies in change detection between the air photo and the satellite image interpretation in fields which were not part of the ESA scheme. The analysis suggested that fields were misinterpreted using both data sources and that in some cases, fields which had appeared to revert to grassland in 1990 were in fact still arable. In addition, farmers outside the ESA agreement had nevertheless converted to grass. In some cases, the availability of five consecutive years of imagery clarified whether apparent changes to grass were permanent.

Visual interpretation of a time series of satellite images is proving to be more accurate for resolving this issue than a single date of air photography or imagery.

BOTANICAL MONITORING

The Pennine Dales ESA covers some 46 000 ha of enclosed grassland (both meadows and pasture) in the upper reaches of river valleys in the mid and north Pennines. One of the principal ESA objectives is to encourage farmers to manage their hay meadows and pastures so that botanical diversity, such as is found in the flower-rich hay meadows, is maintained or improved. In general terms, the more agriculturally improved fields, through more intensive management, are the least botanically rich. One of the main land cover changes of interest within this upland ESA is therefore between grassland types rather than between grassland and other land cover types.

The use of colour air photography to separate improved from unimproved or semi-improved grassland has proved difficult. From detailed botanical data collected on the ground, fields can be allocated to different quality classes, but these data are time consuming to collect and are only available for a sample of fields used for detailed botanical monitoring. Therefore, the use of satellite data was investigated as an alternative or additional means of discriminating grassland types.

To date, monitoring surveys have been undertaken by detailed field survey, recording, in particular, the plant species present. On a broader scale, aerial photography has been used to divide grasslands into coarse land cover classes which reflect the degree of agricultural improvement. This, however, has proved successful only when carried out in conjunction with extensive ground data collection.

A TM image for 14 May 1988 was used. An early spring scene was selected to make use of the greater differentiation in sward growth that typically occurs early in the growing season. Visual inspection of the image suggested that discrimination between grass fields on the basis of more or less productive swards could be possible.

Botanical data had been collected in May and June 1987 for 316 randomly selected fields. All species present within five, 1 m^2 quadrats in each field were recorded.

The parcel statistics utility extracted mean reflectance values and standard errors of these sample fields for all wavebands. In extracting pixel values from the sample fields, boundary pixels were excluded. The botanical data can be treated in a number of ways to derive quantitative indices reflecting conservation value. One of the most promising is a 'nitrogen response' score. A high score reflects a high proportion of species present and is associated with high nitrogen inputs. Low scores, therefore, are associated with swards of higher conservation value.

Botanical indices from the 1987 field data were correlated with the mean reflectance values for all seven TM bands and a Normalized Difference Vegetation Index (NDVI) value for the field from the 1988 image. The NDVI is designed to reflect the amount of green biomass present. The results indicate a significant positive relationship between conservation value and TM bands 3 and 7, and a negative relationship with bands 4 and NDVI. The strongest relationships are found between NDVI and the nitrogen response score.

The underlying relationship reflects the ecological relationship between biomass and conservation value in these marginal upland grass swards. Agricultural management aims to increase productivity and green biomass, usually by high nutrient inputs. Productive swards are dominated by more competitive agricultural species, particularly grasses, which respond most readily to increased nutrient availability. The traditional management which the ESA seeks to encourage is geared towards reducing biomass, particularly through restricting the level of nutrient inputs.

Using TM data, it was possible to discriminate between grassland classes and detect some quite strong relationships between reflectance and botanical characteristics. Data processing in the ways described can produce data which are usable, particularly at the strategic level. This ability to extrapolate from limited field samples is valuable. Strategic spatial information on grassland resource distribution, even at a relatively coarse scale, is often lacking. Spatial resolution is often limiting in the case of the small field sizes in the Dales.

Although the potential to classify grassland types is seen as encouraging, only large grassland changes will be detectable using satellite imagery. Integration of satellite imagery with other GIS datasets, such as altitude, aspect, and soil type, could increase the accuracy of grassland classifications using knowledge-based procedures. This type of approach is only possible within a system which integrates satellite imagery into GIS. This work is reported in more detail by Askew and Slater (1995).

CONCLUSIONS

The suitability of hardware and software for the tasks investigated, especially raster/vector integration with high quality display, is continually changing, but easy-to-use, off-the-shelf packages should soon be available on PC systems.

Overall, the project illustrated the feasibility of using satellite imagery to complement existing data sources rather than replace them. Radar images from ERS-1 were shown to have potential for contributing to land cover change detection. In order to discriminate crops, imagery is required for specific times of the year and analysis is usually unsuccessful if data are acquired for inappropriate dates. Access to a range of imagery is important for conducting work in the UK because of the prevalence of cloud.

The integration of satellite data into botanical models is a viable technique; the spectral sensitivity of satellite imagery was found to relate to the conservation value of grasslands being monitored as a function of biomass.

Not surprisingly, the spatial detail seen within aerial photography is superior to satellite imagery. Nevertheless, the satellite data showed clear advantages in the context of monitoring ESAs. For example, the annual revisit potential of satellite imagery was especially useful for discriminating between permanent grass and grass which was grown as part of an arable rotation. The existence of archived satellite data means that change can be monitored over the past 23 years. The digital nature of satellite data allows them to be processed more readily within GIS than analogue aerial photography.

ACKNOWLEDGEMENTS

BNSC and MAFF funding of the Environmental Monitoring of Protected Landscapes project is gratefully acknowledged.

REFERENCES

Askew, D. and Slater, J. (1995) The use of satellite imagery for assessing the nature conservation value of grasslands. Presented at *IGARSS Conference, 1995, Florence, Italy.*

Slater, J. and Askew, D. (1995) Mapping arable/grassland land cover changes by satellite. Presented at *EN & IN Conference, Budapest.*

Natural Resource Assessment for Nigeria: Using Meteorological Satellite Data to Map Land Cover

Simon I. Hay[1], David J. Rogers[1] and G. R. William Wint[2]

[1]Trypanosomiasis and Land Use in Africa (TALA) Research Group,
Department of Zoology, South Parks Road, Oxford, OX2 3PS, UK.
[2]Environmental Research Group Oxford (ERGO),
Department of Zoology, South Parks Road, Oxford, OX2 3PS, UK.

ABSTRACT

A baseline assessment of land cover against which subsequent changes can be measured and management priorities evaluated is fundamental to achieving a better understanding of the dynamics of natural resource utilization in technologically developing countries. Conventional surveying techniques are expensive, subject to observer bias, and potentially limited by the geography and infrastructure of the country concerned. Remote sensing using public domain meteorological satellite data is, however, largely free from such constraints. In this paper, the application of such satellite datasets to the problem of classifying land cover types in Nigeria is explored. A range of published vegetation indices (RVI, NDVI, SAVI, GEMI) and ground surface temperature algorithms was derived from Pathfinder NOAA-AVHRR data for 1990. Field data of land cover types came from a national aerial survey of land cover in Nigeria performed by Resource Inventory and Management (RIM) in association with the Environmental Research Group Oxford Limited (ERGO) in 1990. Supervised classification of the land cover types was performed by a modified discriminant analysis approach using, as predictor variables, both the raw waveband satellite data and the derived products. Conclusions are drawn on the efficacy of the various indices and algorithms for land cover discrimination and quantification, and on the potential for extending the use of such techniques in space (i.e., predicting land cover in unsurveyed areas) and in time (i.e., the potential for monitoring change).

INTRODUCTION

Land Cover and Natural Resource Management

The term 'land cover' is used to describe the background of naturally vegetated, non-vegetated and human-affected landscapes within a region. In part, these landscapes are themselves the product of large-scale variation in the distribution of soils, temperature, precipitation and edaphic factors. Natural and anthropogenic forces act continuously to modify and change land cover, and it is this shifting mosaic that must be mapped for natural resource management.

The major benefit of mapping the distribution of land cover is to establish a baseline inventory of land cover resources (Meyer and Turner, 1992) with which to develop a better understanding of the factors controlling land cover. This information enables past management decisions to be rationally evaluated, the present situation to be more clearly understood, and future changes to be more effectively predicted. These benefits are especially important in technologically developing regions where land cover information is often inadequate and where ever-increasing human population pressures effect environmental change.

There are, however, substantial problems in acquiring and maintaining accurate information on land cover over large areas. Conventional ground survey techniques are subject to interpreter bias, potential logistical difficulties resulting from local topography and infrastructure and the overall expense of the survey exercise. Aerial photographic techniques can cover large areas rapidly and acquire data on a systematic basis, but they are often prohibitively expensive. By contrast, remote sensing by meteorological satellites can provide a relatively homogeneous sample over extensive geographical areas through a range of spatial, temporal and spectral resolutions depending on the choice of satellite medium (Hay, 1996).

23

Remote Sensing and Land Cover

Existing attempts to map land cover on a broad spatial scale have concentrated on the analyses of low spatial resolution, multi-temporal vegetation indices (Townshend and Tucker, 1984; Tucker *et al.*, 1985; Townshend *et al.*, 1987; Andres *et al.*, 1994; DeFries and Townshend, 1994; Olsson and Eklundh, 1994). These are most commonly derived from data from the Advanced Very High Resolution Radiometer (AVHRR) on board the National Oceanic and Atmospheric Administration's (NOAA) polar orbiting meteorological satellites (Kidwell, 1995). Multi-temporal datasets are favoured because they incorporate information on the seasonal variation of land cover, which is the expression of constituent species phenologies at the biome scale (Fontés *et al.*, 1995).

Early vegetation indices used a simple ratio of AVHRR channel 2 (Ch_2) (near infrared, 0.72–1.10 μm) over channel 1 (Ch_1) (visible red, 0.58–0.68 μm) reflectances called the Ratio Vegetation Index (RVI). The biophysical basis for this relationship is that chlorophyll and carotenoid pigments in plant tissues absorb light in the visible red part of the electromagnetic spectrum, while mesophyll tissue reflects light in the near infrared (Sellers, 1985; Tucker and Sellers, 1986). The problem of reflectance from the (usually dark or reddish) soil background was overcome in later indices by dividing the difference between these two channels by their sum, to give the Normalized Difference Vegetation Index or NDVI:

$$NDVI = \frac{(Ch_2 - Ch_1)}{(Ch_2 + Ch_1)}$$

1

Continuing problems of noise introduced into the NDVI signal by factors such as heterogeneous soil backgrounds (Huete *et al.*, 1985), and differential attenuation of Ch_1 and Ch_2 by atmospheric constituents, provided the impetus to develop 'improved' vegetation indices (Huh, 1991; Jackson and Huete, 1991).

The Soil Adjusted Vegetation Index (SAVI) was developed to minimize interference from the soil background by shifting the intercept of the relationship between Ch_2 and Ch_1 data (Huete, 1988).

$$SAVI = \frac{Ch_2 - Ch_1}{Ch_2 + Ch_1 + L}(1 + L)$$

2

The weighting parameter L varies with vegetation coverage and values of 1.0, 0.75 or 0.25 are recommended for sparse, intermediate and dense vegetation, respectively.

More recently, the Global Environment Monitoring Index (GEMI) has been proposed by Pinty and Verstraete (1992). The GEMI was derived from first principles, although the physical basis for the index is not fully explained in the literature and is defined as follows:

$$GEMI = \eta(1 - 0.25\eta) - \frac{Ch_1 - 0.125}{1 - Ch_1}$$

3

where:

$$\eta = \frac{2(Ch_2{}^2 - Ch_1{}^2) + 1.5Ch_2 + 0.5Ch_1}{Ch_2 + Ch_1 + 0.5}$$

Initial application of the GEMI to African data suggested a three-fold advantage over the NDVI (Flasse and Verstraete, 1994). Firstly, the GEMI was less sensitive to atmospheric variation. Secondly, the influence of clouds was more marked, allowing for more reliable cloud screening regimes, and finally, it had a higher dynamic range in xeric environments, showing details in sparsely vegetated areas that are not visible in other imagery.

The SAVI and GEMI 'improved' vegetation indices have not been widely adopted for land cover mapping. Furthermore, there has only been a limited exploration of the information content of the other AVHRR channels. Data from Channel 4 (Ch_4) (infrared, 10.3–11.3 μm) and Channel 5 (Ch_5) (infrared, 11.5–12.5 μm) can be used to derive information about surface temperature, but a major problem with such measurements is signal attenuation by atmospheric water vapour. The 'split window' technique is used routinely to correct for this effect; by using the greater signal absorption by water vapour in Ch_5, the difference between Ch_4 and Ch_5 in simultaneously recorded images is diagnostic of the degree of attenuation. It is referred to as the 'split window' because it is performed within the same radiance window of the atmosphere. Brightness temperature measurements over land are heavily influenced by surface variation in emissivity (a measure of an object's deviation from black-body emittance at a given wavelength), as well as by the composition and thermal stratification of the atmosphere. Price (1984) proposed a split window algorithm for use over land derived from radiative transfer theory where:

$$T_{surface} = Ch_4 + 3.33\,(Ch_5 - Ch_4)$$

4

Cooper and Asrar (1989) evaluated the performance of this algorithm in tallgrass prairie habitat in Kansas and found it accurate to ±3.0 °C when a constant emissivity value was adopted. Many derivative split window techniques (reviewed by Prata, 1993 and Norman *et al.*, 1995) have been developed which rely largely on ancillary data to quantify atmospheric water content and surface emissivity. The following index based on Becker and Li (1990) attempts a very simple correction for these factors without recourse to ancillary data and has found a preliminary application to multi-temporal vegetation indices of Asia (Gutman, 1993).

$$T_{surface} = Ch_4 + \delta w + \delta \varepsilon$$

5

where:

$$\delta w = 2.63\big((Ch_4 - Ch_5) + 1.274\big)$$

$$\delta \varepsilon = \frac{Ch_4 - Ch_5}{2}\left(0.156 + \left(3.98\left(\frac{Ch_4 - Ch_5}{Ch_4 + Ch_5}\right)\right)\right)\frac{1 - \varepsilon}{\varepsilon}$$

$$\varepsilon = 1.013 + 0.0681\ln(NDVI).$$

The thermal infrared data (Ch_4 and Ch_5) have been applied to land cover classifications both without correction (Achard and Blasco, 1990) and corrected using the Price split window algorithms (Lambin and Ehrlich, 1995a, 1995b). The AVHRR channel 3 (Ch_3) (mid-infrared, 3.55–3.93 μm) is a hybrid of reflected and emitted radiation and has been used to discriminate forest boundaries (Tucker *et al.*, 1985; Kerber and Schutt, 1986; Malingreau *et al.*, 1989; Boyd *et al.*, 1995).

There has, however, been no systematic comparison to date of the discriminatory ability of the alternative vegetation indices and split window algorithms in land cover mapping. A further problem with land cover studies at the regional scale is an objective assessment of product accuracy, generally due to a lack of ground data over such large areas to test predictions (Trodd, 1995). In this investigation, the original raw waveband information, and the potential for land cover discrimination of the range of vegetation indices and split window temperature algorithms described in the introduction, are evaluated. Furthermore, accuracy is assessed using a variety of measures on an extensive Nigerian land cover dataset, and the results are compared with the Anderson criteria for land cover map assessment (Anderson *et al.*, 1976).

METHODS

Ground Data
As part of a World Bank funded national livestock survey, a series of low level systematic reconnaissance flights were made over the whole of Nigeria in 1990. A uniform sampling regime was achieved by flying along gridded transect lines spaced at 20 km intervals (RIM, 1992; Bourn *et al.*, 1994). The whole 924 000 km^2 land area was surveyed between March and April 1990 (i.e., the end of the dry season) and the northern four-fifths of the country, between September and October 1990 (i.e., the end of the wet season). In the dry season, the percentage cover of cultivation, grassland, scrub, woodland, forest and bare ground was estimated from the air. In the wet season, only active cultivation was recorded as the extent of other land cover types did not change significantly. A measure of the accuracy of the technique can be gauged from a comparison of the visual survey data with aerial photographs for active cultivation in Northern Nigeria. They resulted independently in mean percentage cover estimates of 32.5 and 32.05%, respectively (ERGO, 1994).

A Digital Elevation Model (DEM) at 0.083 degree resolution for the whole of Africa was obtained from the Global Land Information System (GLIS) of the United States Geological Survey (USGS), Earth Resources Observation Systems (EROS) data centre. The information for Nigeria was extracted and resampled to an 8 x 8 km resolution for compatibility with satellite data layers.

Satellite Data: Acquisition and Processing
The satellite data were obtained from the Pathfinder AVHRR Land (PAL) dataset of the Earth Observing System Data and Information System at the National Aeronautics and Space Administration's (NASA) Goddard Space Flight Centre (Agbu and James, 1994). These were daily global area coverage (GAC) data for 1990 resampled to a 8 x 8 km resolution in a Goodes Interrupted Homolosine Projection. The daily five channel reflectance data were screened for cloud contamination and pixels were obtained from a view angle greater than 42° using ancillary information provided with the PAL dataset. For exhaustive details on registration, geocorrection, atmospheric correction and cloud screening, see James and Kalluri (1994).

The RVI, NDVI, SAVI and GEMI, and the Price (1984) and Gutman (1993) ground surface temperature estimates, were then calculated. The Gutman (1993) algorithm was modified to incorporate a relationship between NDVI and emissivity derived in Botswana (Van de Griend and Owe, 1993).

$$\varepsilon = 1.0564 \times \ln(NDVI)$$

6

The vegetation and temperature indices and the original five channel data were then individually maximum value composited (MVC) over 10-day periods. Yearly maximum, minimum and mean values were calculated from these decadals for each of the bands. The standard deviation over the year was also calculated to obtain an indication of the annual variability of the signal.

Analysis

The data were subject to a linear discriminant analysis performed using Quick Basic programs written within TALA (by DJR). Datasets using grid squares with a land cover class coverage greater than 50, 60 and 70% were analysed independently in (essentially) a supervised classification exercise in which a different covariance matrix was calculated and used for each vegetation type, and equal prior probabilities were assumed during classification (because the sub-sampled data could no longer be regarded as representative of the whole dataset) (Green, 1978; Tatsuoka, 1971). The 10 variables which gave the greatest separation in multi-variate space between vegetation classes (measured by the summed Mahalanobis distances, called the Mahalanobis Index, within the analysis) were chosen from the 44 processed satellite variables and DEM data. The predicted classification of each pixel was defined by its closeness in multi-variate space (again measured by the Mahalanobis distance) to each of the 'clouds' of pixels representing the different vegetation types, and posterior probabilities were calculated (the latter giving some indication of the likelihood of misclassification). The ability of the discriminant analysis to separate vegetation classes, i.e., the accuracy with which the generated maps predicted survey data, was measured in several ways. First, 'producer' and 'consumer' accuracies were calculated for each vegetation type as the percentage of grid squares within the training set known to have been classified correctly (the producer's accuracy) and the percentage of grid squares assigned to a particular class that actually belonged to that class (the consumer's accuracy). Secondly, the κ (kappa) and τ (Tau) statistics were calculated from the marginal totals of the rows and columns of the classification matrices (the 'error matrices'). These statistics compare the accuracy of the predicted classifications with those expected on the basis of random assignments of each grid square given either the final proportions of grid squares belonging or assigned to a particular vegetation type (i.e., using the *a posteriori* probabilities - κ), or only the proportions of grid squares belonging to a particular vegetation type (i.e., using only the observed *a priori* probabilities - τ). The relative merits and demerits of these two statistics (and formulae for their standard deviations) are given by Ma and Redmond (1995).

RESULTS

Table 1 describes the top 10 variables chosen by the discriminant analysis from the satellite derived and DEM data available at the 50, 60 and 70% dominant land cover class thresholds. Elevation was the most significant descriptor variable in each case, but the raw waveband information from channels 1, 2 and 3, the split window corrected temperatures, and the improved vegetation indices, were all very important. Overall, the accuracy of the analyses increased with higher threshold vegetation coverages, i.e., where the satellite data were presumably increasingly dominated by signals from the chosen vegetation types.

In Table 1, there appears to be a slight tendency for visible and near infrared channels (and their derived products) to dominate in comparison with the thermal channel data (an unsurprising result, given the preponderance of visible/near infra-red channel data and products in the predictor dataset), and this is especially noticeable for the most important variables. Only Ch_3 maximum appears in the top five variables, and that in only one of the three analyses. This result contrasts markedly with the preliminary analyses from this work of the determinants of the distribution of tsetse in West Africa, where thermal variables are frequently very important (Hay, 1995; Rogers *et al.*, in press).

In addition, it is noticeable in Table 1 that while all three maximum, minimum and mean values of the selected channels tend to be chosen with equal frequency, the standard deviations of the same variables (representing variability) are chosen much less often. Only three standard deviations are listed in Table 1 whereas means, maxima and minima appear seven, eight and nine times, respectively.

Table 1. The top predictor variables for Nigeria at 50, 60 and 70% coverages of dominant land cover

Rank	Variable (50%)	Variable (60%)	Variable (70%)
1	Elevation	Elevation	Elevation
2	Ch_1 SD	Ch_1 SD	Ch_2 max
3	Ch_3 max	Ch_1 min	TALA max
4	Ch_1 min	RVI max	GEMI mean
5	RVI mean	NDVI max	GEMI min
6	NDVI mean	SAVI max	Ch_1 min
7	Ch_2 SD	Price mean	Price min
8	Ch_1 mean	GEMI max	RVI min
9	RVI min	Price min	Ch_3 min
10	GEMI max	Ch_2 mean	Price mean
Kappa	0.468	0.541	0.640
Tau	0.467	0.525	0.635

Table 2 gives an indication of the accuracy with which the component land cover types were predicted at the 70% dominant land cover class threshold, and can be interpreted more readily in conjunction with the classification matrix given in Table 3.

Table 2. Classification accuracy of the land cover classes at 70% coverage of dominant land cover

Category	Producer's accuracy (%)	Consumer's accuracy (%)
1. Bare ground	100.0	100.0
2. Grassland	92.9	100.0
3. Scrubland	72.2	61.9
4. Open woodland	50.5	54.7
5. Dense woodland	76.4	68.0
6. Forest	95.2	65.2
7. Mangrove	100.0	100.0
8. All cultivation	72.1	90.8

The classification matrix shows the predicted (columns) against the observed (rows) pixels for each of the land cover classes marked in Table 2. If the statistical description of the ground data was perfect, we should expect all the numbers to appear on the diagonal highlighted in bold. In terms of the Anderson criteria for evaluating land cover classification accuracy and utility (Anderson et al., 1976), the results are encouraging. Though minimum interpretation accuracy falls below 85% in some classes, the overall level of prediction is high and where misclassifications occur, these seem to be understandable; open woodland, for example, is misclassified as dense woodland, dense woodland as forest etc. Furthermore, there are approximately equal accuracies across all the classes and where there are differences, they are more likely to be related to the sample size (e.g. compare bare ground and mangrove with open woodland). Finally, the reasons for the errors in the land cover predictions are reasonably well understood so the present results can be used as a baseline for comparison with future data.

Table 3. A classification matrix for all land cover types at 70% coverage

	1	2	3	4	5	6	7	8	Total
1	3	0	0	0	0	0	0	0	3
2	0	13	0	0	1	0	0	0	14
3	0	0	13	2	0	3	0	0	18
4	0	0	4	52	34	3	0	10	103
5	0	0	2	20	172	23	0	8	225
6	0	0	1	0	2	60	0	0	63
7	0	0	0	0	0	0	11	0	11
8	0	0	1	21	44	3	0	178	247
Total	3	13	21	95	253	92	11	196	684

DISCUSSION

In a review of accuracy assessment in land cover mapping and modelling studies, Trodd (1995) surveyed 84 published land cover classifications based on remotely sensed data between 1994 and 1995. The mean overall percentage of correctly classified pixels was 79.1%, a statistic to which the present results compare favourably, especially since many of the studies utilized high resolution satellite imagery to make predictions at the local scale (Trodd, personal communication). The levels of accuracy with which class estimates can be obtained allow confidence in spatial extrapolation of such predictions to the whole of West Africa for ecological and environmental studies. This is especially important as the 'standard' vegetation maps become increasingly dated and as the rate of environmental change increases.

It was not surprising to find that as the threshold coverage for defining a land cover class increased, so did the ability to predict its occurrence correctly. It highlights, however, the problem of performing such an analysis on spatially heterogeneous land cover. The problem of attempting to define a class on the basis of a pixel whose signal may constitute 50% of that class but, by definition, is composed of 50% of another, needs to be addressed.

The main direction of future research will be the processing of three years' of daily Pathfinder NOAA-AVHRR data for Africa, from which a similar range of indices will be derived. The data will be subject to a temporal Fourier analysis to capture elements of vegetation seasonality more accurately (as detailed in Rogers and Williams, 1994; Andres *et al.*, 1994; Olsson and Eklundh, 1994; Rogers *et al.*, in press). This is of particular interest, given that the temporal variation in the signal (as defined by the standard deviation) was not a good predictor variable for land cover. Though not considered in the present study, the repeat sampling of existing and future geostationary and polar-orbiting satellites offers the opportunity for monitoring changes in land cover in real time (Hay *et al.*, 1996).

Concern is often correctly voiced about the appropriateness of remote sensing techniques to technologically developing regions. Recent changes in the philosophy of satellite data dissemination (Justice *et al.*, 1995) mean that these data have become freely available on request, so the facilities and expertise required for processing the data are now the major limitations. These, however, are becoming less important as computer processing facilities become cheaper in real terms and the level of expertise in the developing regions grows.

CONCLUSION

The objective of the present study was to investigate the extent to which satellite datasets, newly available to the user community, were useful in predicting land cover, whether the accuracies achieved were acceptable, and whether the 'improved' vegetation and split window thermal indices could provide advantages over the raw channel data. The results indicated that natural resource management from meteorological satellite data was feasible, but that a more sophisticated use of the existing remote sensing data was required to achieve accuracies of above 85% across all land cover classes. Given a detailed ground dataset, current public domain satellite data can predict land cover classes to a useful level of accuracy, but extending predictions in both space and time may be problematic.

ACKNOWLEDGEMENTS

The satellite data used by the authors in this study are produced through funding from the Earth Observing System Pathfinder Program of the NASA's Mission to Planet Earth in co-operation with the National Oceanic and Atmospheric Administration. The data were provided by the Earth Observing System Data and Information System, Distributed Active Archive Centre at the Goddard Space Flight Centre which archives, manages and distributes the dataset. Thanks are also due to Mike Packer, Sarah Randolph and David Bourn for useful comments on the manuscript. This work is funded by a grant from the Overseas Development Administration (ODA) administered through the National Resources Institute (NRI) (Project X0239).

REFERENCES

Achard, F. and Blasco, F. (1990) Analysis of vegetation seasonal evolution and mapping of forest cover in West Africa with the use of NOAA AVHRR HRPT data. *Photogrammetric Engineering and Remote Sensing*, **56**: 1359-1365.

Agbu, P.A. and James, M.E. (1994) The *NOAA/NASA Pathfinder AVHRR Land Data Set User's Manual*. NASA. Goddard Space Flight Centre, Greenbelt, Maryland: Goddard Distributed Active Archive Centre Publication.

Anderson, J.R., Hardy, E.E., Roach, J.T. and Witmer, R.E. (1976) A land use and land cover classification system for use with remote sensing data. *United States Geological Survey Professional Paper 964*. Washington: US Government Printing Office.

Andres, L., Salas, W.A. and Skole, D. (1994) Fourier-analysis of multi-temporal AVHRR data applied to land cover classification. *International Journal of Remote Sensing*, **15**(5): 1115-1121.

Becker, F. and Li, Z.-L. (1990) Towards a local split window method over land surfaces. *International Journal of Remote Sensing*, **11**(3): 369-393.

Bourn, D., Wint, W., Blench, R. and Wolley, E. (1994) Nigerian livestock resources survey. *World Animal Review*, **78**: 49-58.

Boyd, D.S., Foody, G.M. and Curran, P.J. (1995) Estimating the biophysical properties of tropical forest canopies using middle infrared radiation: a comparison of reflected and emitted parts. pp. 71-80. In: *Proceedings of the Remote Sensing Society One Day Student Meeting, March 1995, RSS, Leicester.*

Cooper, D.I. and Asrar, G. (1989) Evaluating atmospheric correction models for retrieving surface temperatures from the AVHRR over a tallgrass prairie. *Remote Sensing of Environment*, **27**: 93-102.

DeFries, R.S. and Townshend, J.R.G. (1994) NDVI-derived land cover classifications at a global scale. *International Journal of Remote Sensing*, **15**: 3567-3586.

ERGO (1994) *Land Use Change in Nigeria - 1976-1990*. A report prepared for the United Nations Environmental Programme (UNEP) and the Federal Environmental Protection Agency (FEPA), Abuja, Nigeria.

Flasse, S. and Verstraete, M. (1994) Monitoring the environment with vegetation indices: comparison of NDVI and GEMI using AVHRR data over Africa. pp. 107-135. In: *Vegetation, Modelling and Climate Change Effects*. F. Veroustraete and R. Ceulemans (eds). The Hague, The Netherlands: SPB Academic Publishing.

Fontés, J., Gastellu-Etchegorry, J.P., Amram, O. and Flouzat, G. (1995) A phenological model of the African continent. *Ambio*, **24**: 297-303.

Green, P.E. (1978) *Analyzing Multivariate Data*. Hinsdale, Illinois: The Dryden Press.

Gutman, G.G. (1993) Multi-annual time series of AVHRR-derived land surface temperature. *Advances in Space Research*, **14**: 27-30.

Hay, S.I. (1995) Remotely sensed surrogates of meteorological data for the study of animal species distributions. pp. 24-39. In: *Proceedings of the Remote Sensing Society One Day Student Meeting, RSS, Leicester*.

Hay, S.I., Tucker, C.J., Rogers, D.J. and Packer, M.J. (1996) Remotely sensed surrogates of meteorological data for the study of the distribution and abundance of arthropod vectors of disease. *Annals of Tropical Medicine and Parasitology*, **90**(1): 1-19.

Huete, A.R. (1988) A soil-adjusted vegetation index (SAVI). *Remote Sensing of Environment*, **25**: 295-309.

Huete, A.R., Jackson, R.D. and Post, D.F. (1985) Spectral response of a plant canopy with different soil backgrounds. *Remote Sensing of Environment*, **17**: 37-53.

Huh, O.K. (1991) Limitations and capabilities of the NOAA satellite advanced very high resolution radiometer (AVHRR) for remote sensing of the Earth's surface. *Preventive Veterinary Medicine*, **11**: 167-183.

Jackson, R.D. and Huete, A.R. (1991) Interpreting vegetation indices. *Preventive Veterinary Medicine*, **11**: 185-200.

James, M.E. and Kalluri, S.N.V. (1994) The pathfinder AVHRR land data set - an improved coarse resolution data set for terrestrial monitoring. *International Journal of Remote Sensing*, **15**: 3347-3363.

Justice, C.O., Bailey, G.B., Maiden, M.E., Rasool, S.I., Strebel, D.E. and Tarpley, J.D. (1995) Recent data and information system initiatives for remotely sensed measurements of the land surface. *Remote Sensing of Environment*, **51**: 235-244.

Kerber, A.G. and Schutt, J.B. (1986) Utility of AVHRR channel 3 and 4 in land-cover mapping. *Photogrammetric Engineering and Remote Sensing*, **52**: 1877-1883.

Kidwell, K.B. (1995) *NOAA polar orbiter data users guide (TIROS-N, NOAA-6, NOAA-7, NOAA-8, NOAA-9, NOAA-10, NOAA-11, NOAA-12, NOAA-13 and NOAA-14)*. Washington DC: National Oceanic and Atmospheric Administration.

Lambin, E.F. and Ehrlich, D. (1995a) Combining vegetation indices and surface temperature for land-cover mapping at broad spatial scales. *International Journal of Remote Sensing*, **16**: 573-579.

Lambin, E.F. and Ehrlich, D. (1995b) The surface temperature-vegetation index space for land cover and land-cover changes analysis. *International Journal of Remote Sensing*, **17**(3): 463-488.

Ma, Z. and Redmond, R.L. (1995) Tau coefficients for accuracy assessment of classification of remote sensing data. *Photogrammetric Engineering and Remote Sensing*, **61**: 435-439.

Malingreau, J.P., Tucker, C.J. and Laporte, N. (1989) AVHRR for monitoring global tropical deforestation. *International Journal of Remote Sensing*, **10**: 855-867.

Meyer, W.B. and Turner II, B.L. (1992) Human population growth an global land-use/cover change. *Annual Review of Ecology and Systematics*, **23**: 39-61.

Norman, J.M., Divakarla, M. and Goel, N.S. (1995) Algorithms for extracting information from remote thermal-IR observations of the Earth's surface. *Remote Sensing Environment,* **51**: 157-168.

Olsson, L. and Eklundh, L. (1994) Fourier series for analysis of temporal sequences of satellite sensor imagery. *International Journal of Remote Sensing,* **15**(18): 3735-3741.

Pinty, B. and Verstraete, M.M. (1992) GEMI: a non-linear index to monitor global vegetation from satellites. *Vegetatio,* **101**: 15-20.

Prata, A.J. (1993) Land surface temperatures derived from the advanced very high resolution radiometer and the along-track scanning radiometer 1. Theory. *Journal of Geophysical Research,* **98**: 16 689-16 702.

Price, J.C. (1984) Land surface temperature measurements from the split window channels of the NOAA 7 Advanced Very High Resolution Radiometer. *Journal of Geophysical Research,* **89**: 7231-7237.

RIM (1992) *Nigerian livestock Resources. Four Volumes.* Report prepared by Resource Inventory and Management project (RIM) Ltd to the Federal Department of Livestock and Pest Control Services, Abuja, Nigeria.

Rogers, D.J., Hay, S.I. and Packer, M.J. (in press) Predicting the distribution of tsetse fly species in West Africa using meteorological satellite data. *Annals of Tropical Medicine and Parasitology.*

Rogers, D.J. and Williams B.G. (1994) Tsetse distribution in Africa: seeing the wood and the trees. pp. 249-273. In: *Large-scale Ecology and Conservation Biology. The 35th symposium of the British Ecological Society with the Society for Conservation Biology, University of Southampton, 1993.* Oxford: Blackwell Scientific Publications.

Sellers, P.J. (1985) Canopy reflectance, photosynthesis and transpiration. *International Journal of Remote Sensing,* **6**: 1335-1372.

Tatsuoka, M.M. (1971) *Multivariate Analysis: Techniques for Educational and Psychological Research.* New York: John Wiley & Sons.

Townshend, J.R.G., Justice, C.O. and Kalb, V. (1987) Characterization and classification of South American land cover types using satellite data. *International Journal of Remote Sensing,* **8**: 1189-1207.

Townshend, J.R.G. and Tucker, C.J. (1984) Objective assessment of Advanced Very High Resolution Radiometer data for land cover mapping. *International Journal of Remote Sensing,* **5**: 497-504.

Trodd, N.M. (1995) Uncertainty in land cover mapping for monitoring land cover change. pp. 1138-1145. In: *Proceedings of the 21st Annual Conference of the Remote Sensing Society, 11-14 September, University of Southampton.*

Tucker, C.J. and Sellers, P.J. (1986) Satellite remote sensing of primary production. *International Journal of Remote Sensing,* **7**: 1395-1416.

Tucker, C.J., Townshend, J.R.G. and Goff, T.E. (1985) African land-cover classification using satellite data. *Science,* **227**: 369-375.

Van de Griend, A.A. and Owe, M. (1993) On the relationship between thermal emissivity and the normalized difference vegetation index for natural surfaces. *International Journal of Remote Sensing,* **14**: 1119-1131.

Preparing Natural Resource Managers for GIS

W. H. Erik de Man and Michael J. C. Weir

Department of Land Resource and Urban Sciences, International Institute for Aerospace Survey and Earth Sciences (ITC), 7500 AA Enschede, The Netherlands

ABSTRACT

In many developing countries, the application of GIS to support natural resource management is still hampered by a lack of adequately trained personnel. Increasing use of GIS-based spatial analysis and modelling to support resource management requires that resource managers should be made aware of both the benefits and the pitfalls of GIS technology. Lack of data, poor quality data, and inconsistencies in data derived from different sources, are well-known barriers to the successful implementation of GIS. In developing countries, a range of managerial difficulties and organizational constraints can also seriously impede the implementation of GIS-based resource management. This is a problem particularly at regional and local levels. In this paper, structured approaches to system design and implementation, and techniques for handling data of doubtful quality, are discussed and advocated as important topics for inclusion in education and training courses. These are, however, only partial solutions and do not guarantee the successful implementation of GIS. Approaches for dealing with less tangible, organizational, difficulties are also suggested.

INTRODUCTION

In developing countries whose natural resources provide a major source of income to support development, geographical information systems (GIS) have potential benefits not only as inventory and mapping tools, but also, increasingly, as the basis of spatial decision support systems. However, there are technical, economic, managerial and organizational barriers to the implementation of GIS in developing countries (e.g. Perera and Tateishi, 1995).

The evolution of GIS through the three stages of inventory, analysis and management (Crain and MacDonald, 1984) requires the adaptation and expansion of GIS education and training programmes. In addition to technical (operator) training, the use of a GIS as a management tool creates a need to raise awareness among decision makers, planners and resource managers of both the benefits and the pitfalls associated with the implementation of GIS technology. This awareness is particularly important at regional and local levels in developing countries where GIS users may have to cope alone not only with lack of data, poor quality data and inconsistencies in data derived from different sources, but also with a range of managerial difficulties and organizational constraints. This paper elaborates on these issues.

The paper is divided into four parts. The first part discusses the problem of defining user requirements for geographical information. A structured approach is outlined and illustrated by an example from Indonesia. User information requirements (should!) include some indication of quality. The second part briefly discusses and illustrates the problem of GIS data quality in the context of developing countries. Organizational constraints to the successful implementation and operation of GIS in developing countries are discussed in the third part, and the paper concludes with suggestions for raising awareness of, and coping with, these issues.

IDENTIFYING USER REQUIREMENTS FOR GEOGRAPHICAL INFORMATION: THE INFORMATION UTILIZATION SYSTEM

To be of use, information has to address the requirements of the actual users. These requirements do not exist in isolation but emerge within the context of problem solving. Identification of information requirements must be preceded by a thorough analysis of the problems faced by the user. The purpose of this is to determine what is already known about the problems to be solved, and what is not yet (fully) known and understood. Thus, problem analysis constitutes the scope for the provision of information and supporting information systems. It should result in a better understanding of the user, his responsibilities in decision making and his information requirements. Preferably, therefore, the user community should be involved in the problem analysis.

In most cases, many different actors are involved in problem solving. The information requirements of individuals (or users) therefore have to be integrated with those of others. Problem solving is not usually (completely) novel and *ad hoc*, but involves some elements of routine. This implies that over a period of time, information requirements must be harmonized and integrated into a network of more or less stable information flows. This network of data and information flows, its channels, creators, collectors, users and so on, oriented towards (end) uses, will be referred to as the 'information utilization system' (De Man, 1988).

The identification of user information requirements must begin with the identification of the users and the problems to be addressed. These two activities are not necessarily sequential. UNESCO's *Conceptual framework and guidelines for establishing geographic information systems*' (De Man, 1984) suggests two different approaches to the problem:

- making an inventory of the existing flows and utilization of data and information;
- making an inventory of relevant decision processes and the potential users of information.

The emphasis depends on the orientation of the information management under consideration. For general purpose, supply oriented information handling which is not limited to the execution of (a few) specific functions, the emphasis is on the inventory of the existing flows of data and information (the existing information utilization system) complemented by studies of the relevant decision processes. When dealing with function oriented information handling, the emphasis should be on the analysis of the particular decision processes complemented by an inventory of flows of data (De Man, 1984). The information utilization system provides a framework for identifying, formulating and locating problems and deficiencies in the supply and use of information (De Man, 1988). For this reason, the study of information utilization systems has been found to be an important area of investigation for students from developing countries.

The approach outlined above was used by Susilawati (1990) to investigate the general requirements for spatial information at different levels of management within the Indonesian Ministry of Forestry, and to describe information flows for some typical forest management activities. Forests occupy approximately 1.4 million km^2 (about 80% of Indonesia's land surface) and the forestry sector is a major contributor to the Indonesian economy. The sheer size (31 500 employees) and geographical extent of its operations have led to very complex information flows within the Ministry. Yanuariadi (1991) carried out a detailed analysis of the spatial information required for planning and managing timber estates in Indonesia. The following aspects of forestry agencies at all levels of policy and decision making were examined: management structure; tasks; spatial data/information requirements, collection, processing and production; information utilization; spatial data/information problems and availability; familiarity with GIS. The results were used to prepare matrix structures which summarized the need for, supply, and use of a wide range of spatial data and information by the various agencies.

A structured investigation of the information utilization system identifies information 'gaps' and assesses their effect on the overall functioning of GIS within the organization in question. As the effect of these problems tends to be country- and organization-specific, ready-made solutions are rarely available (De Man, 1988). Some difficulties, however, are shared. One example is the difficulty experienced by resource managers in developing countries, particularly those working at the regional or local level, in obtaining access to existing data such as satellite imagery or aerial photographs. Organizational conditions permitting, sharing of data, facilities and expertise is clearly a solution worth considering.

DATA QUALITY ISSUES

The purpose of information is to reduce uncertainty in management and decision making (De Man, 1988). Although the almost inevitable presence of errors increases uncertainty in spatial data handling (Openshaw, 1989), there is a growing realization that GIS products ought to satisfy appropriate quality standards. In developing countries, however, the cost and time involved in acquiring high quality information is not always reconcilable with the urgency of the demand.

The previous section briefly indicated the enormity of the task of spatial data handling to support forest management in Indonesia. On the islands outside Java, forest land use is regulated by the 'Consensus on Forest Land Use' (TGHK) which allocates forest land to different uses (watershed protection, sustained timber production, conversion to agricultural resettlement) by assigning scores in the area concerned for three factors: slope, soil erodibility and rainfall intensity (Abell, 1988). As it essentially involves simple map overlay, this approach is ideally suited to a GIS-based solution. Weir and Djajono (1994) examined the quality of TGHK classification in a test area in Kalimantan and found the agreement between the official TGHK map and the actual field situation to be only 44%. Although it provided a more detailed classification, thereby removing some local anomalies, simple application of GIS overlay only improved the overall accuracy slightly (55%). The scale and reliability of the basic data used in this GIS analysis were simply inadequate. This research has been used as a simple and salutary case study to illustrate the problems of data quality in typical spatial analysis for natural resource management.

In this particular case, it was possible to develop an error model for indicating the certainty of correct forest land use classification by using relatively high quality, independent surveys to assign probable error values to the basic input data. However, in many developing countries, data to support detailed error modelling are not available. GIS users are then caught in a vicious circle of poor data quality and insufficient benchmark data to support the detailed modelling of this uncertainty. Consequently, they are unable to reach the final 'knowledgeable' phase of GIS application (Coward and Heywood, 1991).

ORGANIZATIONAL ASPECTS

If information is to support planning and decision making, it obviously has to reach the human actors. Information does not flow around in isolation; people generally act in groups and organizations. Consequently, information flows have a dual relationship with prevailing organizational and institutional structures. On the one hand, information flows are governed by the existing organizational set-up, and on the other, the information flows will themselves have an impact on organizational designs.

In fact, information flows are simply part of the communication structures within organizations (information utilization system). In this sense, information interferes with power resources within the organization. To the extent that GIS evolve into analysis and management, the information provided (maps, tables, reports, etc.) becomes strategic. Many examples have shown that a major factor contributing to the success of GIS-based resource management is the ability of the organization to cope with information as a strategic resource. Lack of this ability may easily lead to under-utilization of the rich potentials offered by GIS-technology or, even worse, to adverse effects and organizational frustrations.

Organizational culture often presents a major obstacle to the introduction and application of modern technology. In these cases, the introduction and fruitful application of GIS requires organizational change. Organizational change is, however, a relatively lengthy process and generally takes longer than installing GIS facilities and completing operator training. For this reason, short-term projects involving the establishment of GIS may fail to meet expectations. This problem has been clearly illustrated in Africa. GIS-based resource management is by no means commonplace outside South Africa. One recent survey (Vanderzee and Singh, 1995) indicated that the continent as a whole accounts for only 2% of all GIS and image processing installations worldwide. In spite of this, there has been considerable donor-driven implementation of GIS technology. A survey by Linden (1995) suggested that most of these systems are either not used or do not function optimally. Although there are undoubtedly educational, technical and financial impediments to the implementation of GIS (e.g. Mmono and Kenosi, 1993), Linden suggested that the main reason is lack of appropriate organizational settings.

IMPLICATIONS FOR GIS EDUCATION AND TRAINING

Although prices have declined, the real cost of even a simple PC-based GIS is beyond the means of many resource management agencies in developing countries. While donor agencies can assist by providing equipment, offering user training, and funding surveys to acquire primary data (Olthoff, 1994), the success of GIS in support of natural resource management in these countries ultimately depends on the ability of the agencies involved to use this technology in an efficient and structured way.

In this paper, a number of issues requiring attention in GIS education and training programmes for developing countries has been highlighted. In particular, procedures for structuring information requirements can provide a valuable preliminary to the implementation of GIS, while an appreciation of data quality issues can prevent unrealistic expectations. In this respect, conscious attempts to improve the utilization and quality of information may be therapeutic. A good example is provided by the National LIS/GIS Committee in Zimbabwe. The terms of reference of this committee (Ndambakuwa, 1993) are:

- to establish digital mapping standards;
- to act as an advisory body to users interested in developing LIS/GIS activities;
- to co-ordinate LIS/GIS activities in the country;
- to organize LIS/GIS awareness and facilitate courses and training;
- to submit proposals for a National Policy on LIS/GIS development.

The contextual, mainly organizational and institutional aspects of the introduction and application of GIS mentioned in the previous section are thought to have the furthest reaching implications for training and education programmes. In fact a change can already be seen in the emphasis of GIS training and education programmes from solely technical to contextual issues. This emphasis on the utilization of information and contextual aspects has consequences for the GIS educator whose role will change from instructor to facilitator. It also implies a gradual shift in the role of the GIS expert from technical specialist towards 'agent' of organizational change.

REFERENCES

Abell, T.M.B. (1988) The application of land systems mapping to the management of Indonesian forests. *Journal of World Forest Resource Management*, 3: 111-127.

Coward, P. and Heywood, I. (1991) Aspects of uncertainty in spatial decision making. pp. 233-242. In: *Proceedings of the European Conference on Geographical Information Systems*.

Crain, I.K. and MacDonald, C.L. (1984) From land inventory to land management the evolution of an operational GIS. *Cartographica*, 21(2): 4046.

De Man, W.H.E. (ed.) (1984) *Conceptual Framework and Guidelines for Establishing Geographic Information Systems Capable of Integrating Natural Resources Data and Socio-Economic Data for Development Oriented Planning, Monitoring and Research*. Paris: UNESCO.

De Man, W.H.E. (1988) Establishing a geographical information system in relation to its use – a process of strategic choices. *International Journal of Geographical Information Systems*, 2(3): 245-261.

Linden, G. (1995) Information technology for development. pp. 371-380. In: *Proceedings of the International Conference on Urban Habitat: The Environment of Tomorrow, Delft*.

Mmono, E.N.G. and Kenosi, V. (1993) The state of GIS awareness in the Botswana government machinery. pp. 31-33. In: *Proceedings of the Fourth Seminar on Land and Geographical Information Systems in Zimbabwe, Harare*.

Ndambakuwa, C. (1993) Geographic information systems at the Department of the Surveyor General - past, present and future. pp. 39-43. In: *Proceedings of the Fourth Seminar on Land and Geographical Information Systems in Zimbabwe, Harare*.

Olthoff, W. (1994) GIS in Zimbabwe's public sector: about slow starts, coordination and donor impacts. *GIM: International Journal for Surveying, Mapping and Applied GIS*, 8(5): 32-34.

Openshaw, S. (1989) Learning to live with errors in spatial databases. pp. 263-276. In: *The Accuracy of Spatial Databases*. M. Goodchild and S. Gopal (eds). London: Taylor & Francis.

Perera, L.K. and Tateishi, R. (1995) Do remote sensing and GIS have a practical applicability in developing countries? (including some Sri Lankan experiences) *International Journal of Remote Sensing*, 16(1): 35-51.

Susilawati, S. (1990) *Organizational and operational aspects of geographical information systems for planning and monitoring forest management activities in Indonesia*. MSc thesis [unpublished]. Enschede: ITC.

Vanderzee, D. and Singh, A. (1995) Survey of geographical information system and image processing software. *International Journal of Remote Sensing*, 16(2): 383-389.

Weir, M.J.C. and Djajono, A. (1994) Assessing the accuracy of natural resource data for forest land assessment in Indonesia. pp. 235-242. In: *International Symposium on the Spatial Accuracy of Natural Resource Data Bases, Williamsburg, Virginia.*

Yanuariadi, T. (1991) *The Use of Geographical Information Systems for Industrial Forest Plantation Development in Indonesia.* MSc thesis [unpublished]. Enschede: ITC.

Calibration and Validation of Thematic Maps from Remote Sensing in Developing Countries: Need and Method

J. C. Taylor[1], A. C. Bird[1], C. Sannier[1], N. Pratt[1] and W. Du Plessis[2]

[1]Silsoe College, Cranfield University, Silsoe, Bedford, MK45 4DT, UK.
[2]Etosha Ecological Institute, P.O. Okaukuejo via Outjo, Namibia.

ABSTRACT

Thematic maps derived from satellite image classification and aerial photographic interpretation usually contain significant errors. These result from spectral confusion, mixed pixels, the classification procedure and the scheme of land classification being applied. Experience in the use of thematic classifications for monitoring agriculture in the European Union (EU) has shown the need for statistically designed sample ground surveys to measure classification errors and to compensate for them when using the thematic data. Methodology for calibration and validation of image classifications has been successfully developed and is now widely used for work in Europe. It involves the design of an area-frame sample to select fixed-size areas at random locations in the study area. Land cover maps of the sample areas are then produced by field survey. An unbiased confusion matrix is produced by comparing the field survey with the classification, to show the pattern of error. This, or regression, is applied to obtain area estimates as class pixel counts alone are highly inaccurate. Difficulty of access to randomly selected sites is perceived as a problem when applying the methods in Africa. This work reports surveys of irrigated land area in northern Nigeria and of natural vegetation in Etosha National Park in Namibia where European methods of ground calibration have been tested and successfully adapted for use in the developing world.

INTRODUCTION

The objective of this paper is to draw attention to the need for calibration and validation of thematic maps produced from remote sensing, and to show how methods developed in Europe have been successfully adapted for applications in development projects in Nigeria and Namibia.

Thematic maps from classification of remotely sensed imagery, including aerial photographic interpretation (API), usually contain errors. These can be measured by comparing the thematic map with ground data using a confusion matrix (Story and Congalton, 1986). This is generated by cross-tabulating the frequencies of occurrence of class combinations, obtained from a random double-sample of ground reference data and the classification. As an example, Table 1 presents the confusion matrix generated for a regional crop inventory in the UK in 1992. The overall agreement is the sum of the diagonal elements divided by the total number of observations in the matrix. The off-diagonal row elements represent the mis-classification of ground classes which are included in the image classification. The diagonal element expressed as a percentage of the row total gives the so-called user or mapping accuracy of the classification for that class. The off-diagonal column elements represent the mis-classification of a ground class into other image classes. The diagonal element expressed as a percentage of the column total gives the accuracy that the producer of the classification has achieved for the class. The agreement between a digital classification and ground survey, given by a confusion matrix, is frequently used to estimate its accuracy, assuming the reference data are accurate.

In recent years, considerable experience in the application of remote sensing technology has been gained in the EU's Monitoring Agriculture with Remote Sensing (MARS) project. Digital classifications of Landsat TM and SPOT imagery were carried out over many different parts of the EU and the following observations were made from this collective experience.

Table 1. Confusion matrix showing the relationship between ground survey data and the digital classification of SPOT imagery in the 1992 regional crop inventory of Beds, Cambs and Northants, UK

		Reference Data										
		Woods	Inland Water	Urban	Wheat	Barley	Summer Crops	Grasses	OSR	Other	TOTAL	User Accuracy
	Woods	15	3	1	2	1		2			24	63%
	Inland Water		4		1						5	80%
Image Data	Urban			11			1			1	13	85%
	Wheat	2	1	2	155	8	1	3		1	173	90%
	Barley	8		4	18	16	3	17		3	69	23%
	Summer Crops		1	13		3	43	3	1	5	69	63%
	Grasses			8	6	7	10	37		1	69	54%
	OSR				1				30		31	97%
	Other	2		12	1	3	11	25		16	70	23%
	TOTAL	27	9	51	184	38	69	87	31	27	523	
	Producer Accuracy	56%	44%	22%	84%	42%	63%	42%	97%	59%	Overall Accuracy 63% Kappa 54% Var (kappa) 0.000599	

- The results presented in Table 1 are typical for a classification based on a single image. The overall accuracy was usually between 60 and 75% for classifications having between 8 and 12 classes.
- The overall accuracy tends to be lower as the number of classes increases.
- Accuracy of individual classes is very variable and can be anything between 0 and nearly 100%, depending on spectral separability.
- The accuracy of classifications based on the combination of two or more images is usually improved to about 80–85% for the same numbers of classes mentioned above.

There are several explanations for the occurrence of mis-classification errors.

- Many cover types are botanically and morphologically similar and have very similar reflectance properties. Mis-classification then results from spectral confusion. This is exacerbated when more sub-categories have been included.
- A frequently ignored source of mis-classification is the presence of mixed pixels. These occur along the borders between land parcels of different cover types. The effect of mixed pixels depends on the size of the pixel relative to the parcel sizes. As the size of the pixel approaches the size of land parcels, a very high proportion of the pixels may represent mixtures of all sorts of class combinations. On-going research at Silsoe has shown that in SPOT images of agricultural areas in England, the proportion of mixed pixels was between 13 and 35% (M. J. Dufour, personal communication).
- The digital classification procedure employed also influences the accuracy of classification. The main factors are: the selection process for training data, i.e., how representative the sample is of the spectral

properties of each class; and the classification algorithm used as each one defines the spectral boundaries for each class in a different way.

- The land classification scheme being applied also affects the accuracy of classification which will depend on whether class definitions are based on land cover or land use. In the latter case, variations in land use may be unrelated to spectral differences. Classifications which require separation of classes based on plant species may also be difficult because of the inherent similarity of spectral properties.

The overall accuracy using API is generally higher than for digital classification but there is wide variation in the accuracy of individual classes (Taylor *et al.*, 1991).

The above experience confirms that significant mis-classification errors usually exist in thematic maps produced from remote sensing. This poses important problems for the use of the data:

- as classes are not accurately identified at all locations, and errors vary from map to map, accurate assessment of change by simple cross tabulation of classifications from two dates is not possible;
- estimates of class areas, which are important for agricultural inventory, cannot be accurately measured from pixel counts.

In Table 2, a summary of results from the regional inventory reported by Taylor and Eva (1992) illustrates the latter point and shows the effect of using two different classification procedures. The columns PC-W and PC-UW are the class areas obtained by pixel counts in two separate digital classifications. The columns REG-W and REG-UW are the corresponding areas, and their 95% confidence intervals, estimated by combining the ground survey data with the respective digital classifications using the regression method described by Taylor and Eva (1993). The MAFF column gives, where available, the areas estimated by a census carried out independently by the Ministry of Agriculture, Fisheries and Food (MAFF). Comparison of the area estimates for each cover type shows that the pixel counts are widely different and that they are influenced by varying the digital classification algorithm, hence the degree of mis-classification. On the other hand, the regression estimates are similar to each other and to the MAFF census figures. This shows that the differences caused by varying the classification algorithms have been corrected by the regression technique.

Experience in the use of thematic classifications for monitoring agriculture and natural land cover in the EU has shown the general need to measure classification errors and to compensate for them. The acquisition of an unbiased sample of ground observations of sufficient size is crucial for this so that confusion matrices can be produced or regression estimates made.

The effect of bias can easily be illustrated by examining the effect of over-sampling one class. For example, if we increased the sampling of wheat in Table 1 by a factor of two, we would expect the mis-classifications of the reference data to be in the same proportion. Thus, the wheat column of Table 1 would have every element multiplied by two. This would increase the estimate of the user accuracy of wheat to 95%. However, the user accuracies for the other classes would be under-estimated because of the increased number of wheat commission errors. The user accuracy of barley for example would be reduced to 18%.

The confusion matrix will be biased if the samples for each class are not proportional to the class areas. As these are not known before the classification, a random sample design is used to obtain the necessary data. The MARS project

Table 2. Areas (ha) of cover types in the same region of England estimated by different techniques using digital classifications and by agricultural census

CLASS	PC-W[1]	PC-UW[2]	REG-W[3]	REG-UW[4]	MAFF[5]
Woodland	35153	42834	29636 ±19%	29409 ±25%	na
Inland water	5510	4123	5744 ±58%	6279 ±44%	na
Urban	111775	22518	82594 ±14%	70668 ±20%	na
Wheat	210459	159938	238003 ±6%	236736 ±6%	227637
Barley	22839	93969	53900 ±27%	55502 ±24%	50585
Summer crops	66990	105593	89888 ±13%	96494 ±15%	82587
Grass and forage	192582	107509	130339 ±12%	124691 ±13%	114491
Rape	29946	29047	44244 ±10%	44095 ±11%	46643

[1]pixel count, area-weighted discriminant functions; [2]pixel count, un-weighted discriminant functions; [3]regression estimate, area-weighted discriminant functions; [4]regression estimate, un-weighted discriminant functions; [5]MAFF agricultural census

employed an area-frame sample, developing methods used by USDA for crop area estimation in the 1970s (Hanuschak *et al.*, 1979). Between 1988 and 1993, there were study sites in 10 countries, generally covering areas of around 20 000 km². The study regions were divided into fixed-size areas by a regular grid to produce the sampling frame. Random samples of the fixed-size areas (referred to as segments) were selected. Many of the MARS study sites used a stratified sample design. All the sample segments were visited in the field to identify and map each land parcel within the segment. This required that the enumerators were suitably trained in the identification of crops and other land cover classes, and were equipped with suitable documents to enable them to locate the segments and draw maps of sufficient accuracy in the field. For example, the survey documents for each segment in the UK study consisted of: a false colour composite satellite imagette of the 1 km square segment and the surrounding 0.5 km border at 1:10 000 scale; a transparent 1:10 000 OS overlay of the segment and surrounding area; a 1:25 000 map of the segment and surroundings; a transparent overlay on which to draw parcel boundaries; a proforma on which to record parcel numbers and crop types; and a 1:50 000 OS map of the area for road navigation.

Area-frame sampling was successfully used in Libya by Latham *et al.* (1983) to measure irrigated areas, but its general application in Africa is perceived as being limited. The requirement for a random sample of locations generally means that access will be very difficult for some sites. The temptation is to ignore these even though doing so would invalidate the error assessment. The following are two examples of applications of area-frame sampling in Africa where feasible methods have been developed.

VEGETATION MAPPING IN ETOSHA NATIONAL PARK

Classification of vegetation in Etosha National Park was carried out as part of a project to measure vegetation status in near real time using NOAA-AVHRR images (Sannier *et al.*, 1995). The classification scheme used in Etosha was adapted from the Yangambe classification (Boughey, 1957) and aimed to separate vegetation classes according to the height, density and main species of woody vegetation.

A randomly aligned, systematic area-frame sample was chosen to facilitate aerial as well as ground survey. The sampling frame was the Universal Transverse Mercator (UTM) grid and the sample segments were 1 km square. The location of one sample segment within a 10 x 10 km block was determined randomly to give a 1% sampling rate, and the same location was used within each adjacent block to give the systematic sample of 220 segments inside the Park as shown in Figure 1. Three types of field survey documents were produced, based on geo-referenced Landsat TM imagery map products. These were: 1:125 000 scale image maps of the whole Park, in sheets covering 20 x 20 km, to assist navigation; 1:30 000 scale extracts, covering a 4.5 x 4.5 km area centred in each segment, to locate them; and 1:10 000 scale extracts of the segments for mapping. In addition, surveyors were supplied with booking forms, which included the class definitions for ready reference in the field, to help maintain consistency of class identification.

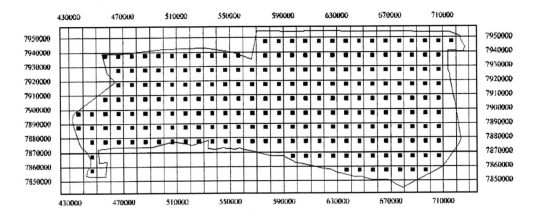

Figure 1. Area-frame sample of Etosha National Park

A total of 82 sites were surveyed on the ground and all sites were surveyed from the air. The ground survey was implemented in order to check the air survey. Prior to the field/aerial visit, the 1:10 000 TM extracts were photo-interpreted and parcel boundaries were drawn on to acetate overlays. On the ground, the position within the segment was determined by a GPS (Global Positioning System). This instrument was indispensable because there were no features to assist navigation most of the time. Parcel boundaries were checked and modified when necessary. The vegetation type of each parcel was determined and recorded on the booking form. From the air, the plane was navigated by the GPS to each site at a local altitude of 200–250 m and a speed of 120 kn. One observer recorded the vegetation with the help of the field survey documents, while another filmed the site through the window using a standard camcorder. After the flight, the video was used to verify the interpretation made in the plane. All segments were surveyed in about 30 h of flying; ground survey took about 10 times as long.

A random sub-sample of the survey data was used to derive spectral signatures for 33 land cover classes. The number of training pixels for each class was made approximately proportional to the class areas. Some of the classes had multimodal statistical distributions and were sub-divided using a clustering routine. The classification was performed using the maximum likelihood algorithm. Two TM images covering the east and west of the Park were classified separately and the classifications were mosaiced later.

A confusion matrix was produced from the random sub-sample of survey locations. This enabled the agreement of the classification with survey data to be calculated for different levels of class groupings. Table 3 is the confusion matrix for seven main classes and shows that the overall agreement was 68%. Savanna cover types can be difficult to classify because boundaries between classes are often diffuse. The confusion matrix reflects this. Comparison of the ground survey and air survey results, also in a confusion matrix, indicated the classes which could not be reliably discriminated by visual assessment. Some types of mis-classifications were judged to be unimportant for the production of vegetation status maps and when these cases were allowed for, the agreement rose to over 80%. The confusion matrix will allow the digital classification to be used for various purposes as quantitative assessment of the errors can be made.

Table 3. Matrix for Etosha vegetation survey

Classification	Reference Data							Total	User Acc
	1	2	3	4	5	6	7		
1 Bare Ground	2454	21	1		1	11		2488	99%
2 Grassland	54	140	16	5	62	15	12	304	46%
3 Steppe	46	75	407	48	46	35		657	62%
4 Grass Savanna		2	13	50	74	46	4	189	26%
5 Shrub Savanna	17	23	34	21	1824	793	82	2794	65%
6 Low Tree Savanna	1	16	6	2	932	1539	151	2647	58%
7 High Tree Savanna		6			284	363	687	1340	51%
Total	2572	283	477	126	3223	2802	936	10419	
Producer Acc	95%	49%	85%	40%	57%	55%	73%	Overall Acc	68%

ESTIMATING THE AREA OF SMALL-SCALE IRRIGATION IN NORTHERN NIGERIA

An agricultural monitoring project was carried out in the region of northeast Nigeria adjacent to the border with Niger as part of the programme reported by Bird *et al.* (1995). The study area presented a complex agricultural setting with dryland agriculture on better drained sands, and various forms of flood-related or irrigated cultivation in the floodplain areas (Kimmage and Adams, 1990). In this study, the area of land under irrigation was the main focus. The aim of the project was to test the methodology which might be appropriate to the area in order to produce same-season inventory figures. For this reason, the study was based on those areas of irrigation which could be covered by one SPOT XS satellite image. The actual region studied was restricted to zones where small-scale irrigation was known to be feasible. Two zones were defined around the river system which was the main water source. These were delineated from a grid of 500 x 500 m squares overlaid on photomosaics created from aerial photographs independently of this work. Squares which contained a potential surface water resource, such as the river, a channel or a pond, were allocated to zone 1, while the squares adjacent to these were allocated to zone 2. This led to a study area of 252.5 km^2 within the SPOT scene. A field survey was designed, based on a sample size of 500 x 500 m, using an unaligned systematic random sample with a sampling fraction of 5%. This amounted to 49 ground segments, each of which was mapped during the field survey. The field survey was carried out during 10–24 January 1994, which coincided with the peak of the irrigation season. A SPOT satellite image was acquired on 11 January 1994.

Within the study area defined by the image, the first zone contained 32 segments, of which 11 included irrigation sites; the second zone had 17 segments of which only three contained irrigation. A supervised classification was applied to the imagery with training pixels derived from the ground survey data. The training was based on a simple irrigation/non-irrigation scheme. The classification was carried out using two of the available algorithms, 'maximum likelihood' and 'k nearest neighbour', on the ILWIS software package (ILWIS, 1993). Low mapping or user accuracies were found for the irrigated area in the order of 40% for 'maximum likelihood' and 30% for 'k nearest neighbour'. Confusion occurred between irrigation, woodland and aquatic grassland, i.e., between those classes made up of green vegetation. The 'k nearest neighbour' method classified twice as many pixels as the 'maximum likelihood' method. The predicted locations of irrigation were the same, but the number of pixels classified in those locations differed. The resulting maps could be used as general indicators of where irrigation was likely to occur but not as accurate maps. Quantitative data were better derived from area estimates for the study area as a whole.

The area of irrigated land could be calculated in a number of ways from the data collected. The options were: direct expansion of the field data; pixel counting from the classified image; or the application of the regression estimator using both the field data and the image classification. Table 4 summarizes the results obtained from these techniques. The direct expansion of field data gave a wide confidence interval while the pixel count showed major differences between the two classification methods. By applying the regression estimator technique, the two classifications yielded much more comparable results. For both zones, it could be said that between 469 and 1107 ha of irrigation exist in a study area of 25 250 ha, or between 1.9% and 4.4%.

The results of this work indicated that first estimates of the area under small-scale irrigation could be made in a study area where previously, no information was available. The estimates were far from exact numbers, but were upper and lower limits of a range. They provided a starting point for land use planning with regard to irrigation and water supply in the area.

Table 4. Estimated area of small-scale irrigation

Total study area	25 250 ha
Irrigated area– by direct expansion of field data	840 ± 524 ha
Irrigated area– by classified image pixel count 'maximum likelihood' classifier 'k nearest neighbour' classifier	1009 ha 2312 ha
Irrigated area – by regression estimator 'maximum likelihood' classifier 'k nearest neighbour' classifier	788 ± 319 ha 749 ± 369 ha

CONCLUSIONS

The work in Africa has confirmed that field surveys which enable the collection of statistically unbiased data can be implemented in Africa. The use of GPS to locate sample sites has facilitated the collection of land cover data from aircraft in otherwise inaccessible locations. Data collection by ground survey was feasible but more time consuming.

The digital classifications carried out in Namibia and Nigeria contained similar problems to those in the MARS project, namely, high levels of mis-classification. Area estimates made from pixel counts alone depended on the classification algorithm used and were unreliable. The integration of an area-frame sample of ground survey data with results of digital classification led to more consistent estimates.

Proper calibration of digital classifications with statistically unbiased ground data is both necessary and feasible in Africa. The methods developed in the EU have been successfully adapted for this.

REFERENCES

Bird, A.C., Pratt, N.D. and Lawan, A.I. (1995) The development of GIS and remote sensing techniques in the Centre for Arid Zone Studies, North East Nigeria. Presented at *Remote Sensing and GIS for Natural Resource Management, RSS Workshop, 19 December 1995, Chatham, UK.*

Boughey, A.S. (1957) The physiognomic delimitation of West African vegetation types. *Journal of the West African Science Association,* **3**(2): 148-165.

Hanuschak, G., Sigman, R., Craig, M., Ozga, M., Luebbe, R., Cook, P., Kleweno, D. and Miller, C. (1979) *Obtaining Timely Crop Area Estimates Using Ground-Gathered and Landsat Data. USDA Technical Bulletin,* no. 1609. Statistical Research Division, Economics Statistics and Co-operative Services, USDA.

ILWIS (1993) *ILWIS User's Manual.* Enschede, Netherlands: International Institute for Aerospace Survey and Earth Sciences.

Kimmage, K. and Adams, W.M. (1990) Small-scale farmer-managed irrigation in northern Nigeria. *Geoforum,* **20**: 435-443.

Latham, J.S., Ferns, D.C., Colwell, J.E., Reinhold, R. and Jebe, E.H. (1983) Monitoring the changing areal extent of irrigated lands of the Gefara Plain, Libya. *Advances in Space Research,* **2**(8): 57-68.

Sannier, C., Taylor, J.C., du Plessis, W. and Campbell, K. (1995) Application of remote sensing and GIS for monitoring vegetation in Etosha National Park. Presented at *Remote Sensing and GIS for Natural Resource Management, RSS Workshop, 19 December 1995, Chatham, UK.*

Story, M. and Congalton, R.G. (1986) Accuracy assessment: a user's perspective. *Photogrammetric Engineering and Remote Sensing,* **52**: 397-399.

Taylor, J.C., Bird, A.C., Keech, M.A. and Stuttard, M.J. (1991) *Landscape Change in the National Parks of England and Wales - Final Report. Vol. 1. Main Report.* Silsoe College, Bedford.

Taylor, J.C. and Eva, M.D. (1992) *Regional Inventories on Beds, Cambs and Northants (UK).* Final Report. Contract No. 4817-92-06 ED ISP GB Joint Research Centre, Commission of the European Communities. Silsoe College, Silsoe.

Taylor, J.C. and Eva, M.D. (1993) Operational use of remote sensing for estimating crop areas in England. In: *Towards Operational Applications. Proceedings of the 19th Annual Conference of the Remote Sensing Society, Chester, UK, 1993.* Nottingham: Remote Sensing Society.

Techniques In Electronic Imaging For Natural Resource Monitoring

Alexander Koh, Esther Edwards, Richard Curr and Fiona Strawbridge

RSGIS Unit, Bath College of Higher Education, Newton Park, Bath, BA2 9BN, UK.

ABSTRACT

Increasing importance is placed on the need to match properties of the land with its use and management to ensure economic and environmental sustainability. The ability to deal effectively with problems and issues as they arise requires near real time availability of objectively measured, quality information. It is important that these data can be readily processed and integrated with other data from different sources to produce output which is rapidly and easily accessible and comprehensible. Remote sensing techniques are capable of fulfilling this mandate. This paper discusses two different techniques in electronic imaging, Airborne Digital Photography (ADP) and High Resolution Videography (HRV), which have been used to acquire information for natural resource management in two diverse application areas. Their relatively low-cost, fly-on-demand capability, ability to operate below cloud cover, and high spatial resolution, enables the ADP and HRV systems to cover large expanses of landscape in a very short time and to deliver timely digital data. This makes them invaluable tools for environmental and resource monitoring and management, particularly when integrated into a Geographic Information System (GIS). The ADP system has been used in multi-spectral mode to monitor land degradation and rehabilitation in a semi-arid environment in Baringo District, Kenya. The HRV system has been used to monitor change on a sand dune system in the UK. The technical aspects which must be considered prior to utilizing such systems are examined.

INTRODUCTION

Earth observing satellites are powerful tools for the remote sensing of the earth's surface at both continent and nationwide scales, but they are all disadvantaged by their poor to modest spatial resolution and/or inappropriate timeliness. Relating measurements in the field to AVHRR data with a nominal ground pixel resolution of 1 km is very difficult, and even at the resolution of SPOT Panchromatic with a nominal ground pixel resolution of 10 m, the lack of detail can be a severe hindrance to mapping and analysis. Large format aerial photography is a very suitable intermediate data source, but it is often either unavailable or expensive to obtain; furthermore, it is normally in analogue form and has limited spectral resolution.

The ADP and HRV systems provide versatile and inexpensive alternatives to traditional forms of satellite imagery and aerial photography. They also have the benefits of timeliness and spectral compatibility with images acquired from current earth observation systems, as the spectral sensitivity of both sensors spans the entire range of visible light and extends well into the near infrared.

Image interpretability is dependent on the ground resolution of the pixels and the dimensions of the features being analysed. For features with dimensions approaching, or less than, the ground pixel resolution, interpretation is a demanding task. Image resolution can be placed into three categories: the recognition of classes, the identification of features, and the analysis of objects. At the first level for example, the image interpreter can recognize broad categories of land class; at the second level, the user can identify features within a class, and at the third level, the remote sensor should be able to analyse objects within these features. The data obtained from both ADP and HRV, with typical nominal ground pixel resolutions of better than 0.15 m (ADP) and 0.5 m (HRV), deliver all three resolution categories, enabling the remote sensor to recognize, identify and analyse images. Figure 1 shows three greyscale images of the UK. The upper image is part of a single band NOAA scene with 1 km resolution. Here, the land mass of the UK is clearly recognizable, as are regions of upland and lowland and major cities, although it is not possible to identify any individual features within the image. The central image is part of a Landsat TM, band 3 (0.63–0.69 μm) scene at 30 m resolution showing part of the north Cornwall coast. In this image, it is possible to identify specific features within a land class such as fields and field boundaries, roads, rivers, beaches, etc. The lower image is an HRV red band (0.62–0.69 μm) mosaic at 50 cm resolution, showing the area of coastline outlined in the Landsat scene. Here, the landform can be readily identified as a sand dune system, and because of the very high spatial resolution obtainable by HRV, it is possible to analyse the image for object details such as vegetation units, areas of bare sand, fence lines and paths.

Figure 1. Level 1 Recognition, Level 2 Identification, Level 3 Analysis

ELECTRONIC IMAGING DEVICES

There are fundamental differences in image capture, storage, manipulation and transmission between photographic and electronic imaging devices. Conventional aerial cameras use photographic film for recording images which must be processed chemically to reveal the acquired image. These images are often stored as hard copy. In contrast, digital cameras, often referred to as still video cameras, use a camera body and lens but record the image with charge-coupled devices (CCD). The images thus acquired are stored in digital format, usually on computer disks. Digital cameras have, until very recently, required permanent connection to a computer for power supply, image acquisition and storage. Technological advances have allowed the development of completely independent cameras which carry an internal power supply and storage medium (Peipe and Schneider, 1995). Several digital cameras are now available commercially (Bosemann *et al.*, 1994). High resolution videography is electronic imaging whereby standard television signals are recorded on magnetic media. The stored image data are in analogue form and as such are not readable by a computer. It is therefore necessary to convert this analogue signal to a digital signal using an Analogue to Digital (A-D) converter. The cameras used for HRV can be single-band cameras, multiple single-band cameras or multi-band cameras. HRV systems using single-band cameras are capable of sensing electromagnetic radiation within a pre-defined range of wavelengths, for example, 0.63–0.69 μm (red). Systems using multiple single-band cameras are capable of sensing within two or more pre-defined wavelengths, for example, 0.63–0.69 μm (red) and 0.76–0.90 μm (near infrared). Multi-band cameras are capable of sensing several parts of the electromagnetic spectrum at the same time, for example, 0.52 μm (green) to 0.90 μm (near infrared).

HRV System Components

The HRV system designed in the RSGIS Unit comprises one or more lightweight video cameras, mounted vertically in a light aircraft, with associated video tape recorders and video monitor (Figure 2). Each camera lens unit is fitted with a homologous glass filter which allows the required wavelengths to pass and strike the CCDs. The CCD has dimensions of 6.4 mm (H) x 4.8 mm (V) and consists of 732 (H) x 290 (V) picture cells. Using the frame-transfer method, this produces 699 (H) x 576 (V) active picture elements. The field of view of the cameras and the sighting of ground targets is controlled by the use of a cockpit-mounted video monitor which displays the radiometrically sensitive, real time image. This enables the pilot to follow pre-planned flight lines to meet mission coverage requirements. The continuous terrain view is recorded in analogue form on SVHS tapes which become immediately available for analysis and interpretation.

Figure 2. HRV system located in a light aircraft

The archived analogue video data can be digitized using an imaging board. These frames can then be exported to be used as back-drops in GIS, in remote sensing and imaging processing systems, or to create hard copy. As the demand for integrating remotely sensed data with other data types expands, geometric registration of these images is becoming increasingly important. Ground control can be difficult to achieve in many natural environments because they are usually dynamic in nature, sometimes inaccessible, and often lack previously documented static targets. The collection of positional data using Global Positioning Systems (GPS) is emerging as a promising solution, enabling rapid collection of latitude, longitude and altitude data. To this end, two GPS receivers have been incorporated into the HRV system to allow differential positioning. A diagrammetric representation of the system is shown in Figure 3.

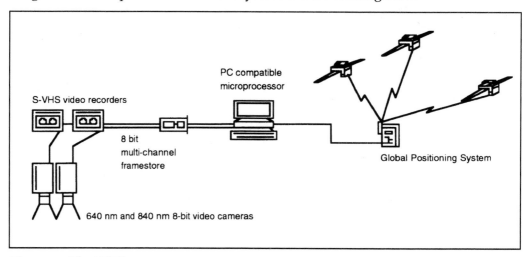

Figure 3. The HRV system

The HRV system will operate between −10°C and +50°C, from sea level to 3048 m above sea level, and up to a non-condensing r.h. of 95%. Mechanically, the system is capable of withstanding shock of 15 g and vibration at 5–60 Hz with 2.08 mm total excursion, or 30 g in any axis under non-operating conditions.

Airborne Digital Photography

Although airborne digital photography using cameras such as the Kodak DCS 420 has not been tested extensively, it is already emerging as a promising technique in electronic imaging for landcover analysis (Fraser, 1994; King *et al.*, 1994). For some applications, there are several advantages over video. One significant advantage is that digital cameras are not subject to national video input and output standards, so the array size of the CCD can be greater than that of video cameras; a typical array size is 1524 (H) x 1012 (V), allowing an increase in area ground cover/ frame. The major constraint on any further increase in resolution is increase in file size (a two-fold increase in resolution results in a four-fold increase in file size) and hence, increased data handling time and data storage capacity requirements. The output from the CCD chip is written directly to a digital storage medium on board the camera rather than to video tape; this results in less re-sampling of data and hence, superior image resolution. The digital images so produced are immediately available for image processing operations to enable image enhancement and analysis.

The Airborne Digital Photography (ADP) System Components

The ADP system is based on the Kodak professional DCS 420 digital camera (Figure 4) which combines portability with ease of use as it can be operated like a small format film-based camera. The system comprises one or more cameras mounted vertically in a light aircraft and integrated with an electronic power management and shutter release control unit. The control unit is programmable to 0.01 s to enable capture of stereo imagery for a pre-determined altitude, focal length and image resolution. The camera(s) is mounted on a chassis with integrated shock and vibration absorbers which conform to MIL-E-5400 and AIR 7303 military characteristics standards. It carries an electronic back, in place of the 35 mm film, fixed to the body of a modified Nikon N90 camera. The camera accepts all the F-mount lenses offered for the N90. The CCD has a 9 μm square picture cell arranged in a 1524 (H) x 1012 (V) array, producing 1.5 million pixels in monochrome mode. The CCD pickup area of 13.8 mm (H) x 9.2 mm (V) results in a photosensitive area 2.6 times smaller than that of film (36 mm (H) x 24 mm (V)), giving rise to a corresponding reduction in viewing angle.

Figure 4. The centre of the ADP system is the Kodak DCS 420 digital camera

A framing rate of 3 images/s is possible to allow digital stereo coverage. These images are then stored on a 260 Mb capacity Type 3, PCMCIA-ATA standard removable hard disk which allows storage of up to 162 images at a rate of 1 frame/2.75 s. Each camera lens unit can be fitted with a filter, with end user-defined band passes and peak responses, to produce customized imagery for specialist applications. This system will operate within a temperature range of +5°C to +50°C, from sea level to 3048 m above sea level, and up to a non-condensing r.h. of 85%. Mechanically, the system is capable of withstanding shock of 100 g under operational conditions. The storage device has a built-in shock sensor which prevents information being overwritten in the event of shock during data transfer. The automatic head lock parks the heads in the landing zone when the drive is removed.

THE APPLICATION OF ADP AND HRV
Through their relatively low-cost, fly-on-demand capability, ability to operate below cloud cover and high spatial resolution, the ADP and HRV systems

provide sources of complementary data for current earth observation satellites. The high spatial resolution of 0.5 m/ pixel or better is a useful tool for validating satellite data and enhancing their thematic mapping capability. When satellite scenes are affected by small amounts of cloud cover, these systems also provide useful information on how the scene may be repaired. Application areas of the HRV and ADP systems have included change detection on sand dune systems and monitoring land degradation and rehabilitation in semi-arid environments.

Change Detection on Sand Dunes using HRV

Sand dunes are an important natural phenomenon and are now recognized as a cost-effective, environmentally sound, natural coastal defence. They also play an important role in regulating coastal groundwater (Louisse and Van der Meulen, 1991) and provide a habitat for a rich community of highly specialized plant and animal species (Carter, 1988). There is now firm evidence that more than half the sand dune systems in the UK are moving landward, and that most of the remainder are stationary, rather than growing seaward (English Nature, 1992). Anthropogenic erosion is a very significant threat to sand dunes. The major impact results from the recreational use of dunes which destroys the vegetation and exposes the sand to aeolian and marine attack. The resultant blow-outs can cause the loss of large areas of the dune system (Doody, 1982). Interest in the factors which control the stability of dunes has been renewed with an increased tendency towards 'soft' engineering strategies as opposed to 'hard' approaches involving expensive sea walls and groynes. The dynamic nature and spatial extent of sand dunes make it costly and difficult to continuously monitor the performance of these systems, using conventional methods, when under stress from natural and anthropogenic pressures. HRV can be used for rapid, cost-effective data acquisition. Figure 5 shows two red band HRV images, with 50 cm ground pixel resolution, of the same section of a sand dune system. The images were acquired in October 1993 (a) and one year later in October 1994 (b). Vegetated areas appear black whereas areas of bare sand appear pale grey. These two images provide conclusive evidence of complete erosion of some areas of dune vegetation (image b). Over the course of one year, the consequent increase in the area of bare sand, and the increase in the number of footpaths intersecting the dune surface, demonstrate the potential of this technique for monitoring change through time.

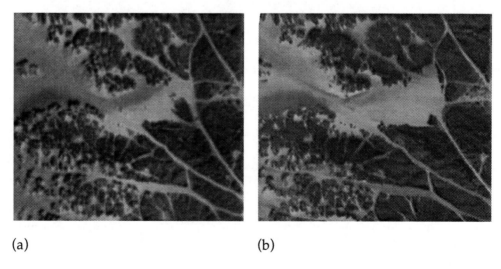

(a)   (b)

Figure 5. HRV red band images showing change through time

Monitoring Land Degradation and Rehabilitation in a Semi-Arid Environment Using ADP

Despite decades of research into the processes involved in soil erosion and conservation techniques, soil loss remains a fundamental problem in semi-arid environments. The ADP system has been used as a cost-effective tool for identifying areas susceptible to erosion, planning remedial works, enhancing water harvesting, slowing down erosion where it exists, and then for evaluating the effect of constructing soil and water conservation structures. Figure 6 shows an infrared band ADP image with 15 cm ground pixel resolution, imaged from 300 m AGL. The image shows part of a farm, sited on the alluvial plain between the escarpment which lies to the west of Lake Baringo, Kenya, and the lake itself.

The gently sloping alluvial plain has suffered severe loss of vegetation through over-grazing and poor cultivation techniques which have ravaged the natural flora and diminished the bush vegetation to such an extent that soil erosion is now a major problem. The average annual precipitation is about 600 mm but this is usually high intensity, sporadic rainfall which results in surface run-off and the loss of topsoil. This image shows an extensive network of gullies cutting back into the cultivated land. Soil and water conservation structures, in the form of tied ridging, have been constructed inside the field boundaries to increase infiltration and reduce surface run-off and rill formation. High resolution ADP images of the type shown here can be used to monitor progress in the development of the gully system, and the degree to which the conservation techniques have arrested the development of rills and gullies.

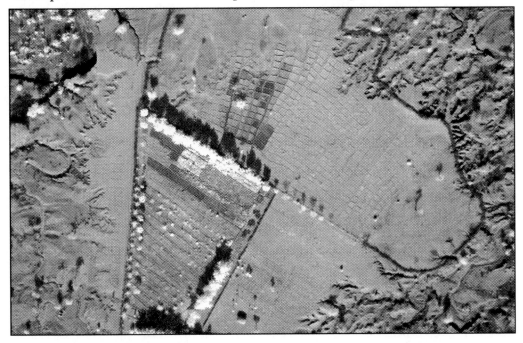

Figure 6. ADP infrared image of gully erosion in a semi-arid environment

Other examples of the complementary role of ADP and HRV systems include soil moisture analysis (Everitt et al., 1989), monitoring coastal zone processes (Eleveld and Jungerius, 1993), land cover classification (Nixon et al., 1985; Marsh et al., 1994), natural and commercial forest resource management (King and Vlcek, 1990), monitoring of arable crop performance and hectarage (Manzer and Cooper, 1982; Everitt et al., 1991; Escobar et al., 1983), local area mapping (Fraser and Shortis, 1995), the determination of elevation for digital elevation models (King et al., 1994), validating savanna burn scars and validation of earth observation satellite data (work in progress), and monitoring footpath and road traffic flow volume and patterns (work in progress). Further possibilities might include: hydrological surveys, geomorphic mapping, flood plain and saturated soil zonation, and monitoring of urban and peri-urban growth. It is anticipated that future technological improvements in both sensor resolution and on-board storage capability will result in even broader use of airborne digital imaging and high resolution videography.

ACKNOWLEDGEMENTS

The authors acknowledge the Natural Resources Institute for funding research and development of the ADP System, and for funding data collection in Baringo, Kenya, under project number X0286 LARST Airborne Videography for High Resolution Environment Mapping and Monitoring.

REFERENCES

Bosemann, W., Peipe, J. and Schneider, C.-T. (1994) Zur Anwendung von Still Video Kameras in der Digitalen Nahbereichsphotogrammetrie. *Zeitschrift fur Photogrammetrie und Fernerkundung,* **63**(3): 90-96.

Carter, R.W.G. (1988) *Coastal Environments* 617. London: Academic Press.

Doody, P. (1982) *The Conservation of Sand Dunes.* UK: Nature Conservancy Council.

Eleveld, M.A. and Jungerius, P.D. (1993) *The use of GRASS for the classification of video images applied to geomorphological processes in the coastal dunes of Schouwen.* Internal Report, Department of Physical Geography and Soil Science, University of Amsterdam, The Netherlands.

English Nature (1992) *Coastal Zone Conservation - English Nature's Rationale, Objectives and Practical Recommendations.* UK: English Nature.

Escobar, D.E., Bowen, R.L., Gausman, H.W. and Cooper, G.R. (1983) Use of near infrared video recording system for the detection of freeze damaged citrus leaves. *Journal of the Rio Grande Valley Horticultural Society,* **36**: 61-66.

Everitt, J.H., Escobar, D.E., Alaniz, M.A. and Davis, M.R. (1989) Using multispectral video imagery for detecting soil surface conditions. *Photogrammetric Engineering and Remote Sensing,* **55**: 476-471.

Everitt, J.H., Escobar, D.E., Villarreal, R., Noriega, J.R. and Davis, M.R. (1991) Airborne video systems for agricultural assessment. *Remote Sensing Environment,* **35**: 231-242.

Fraser, C.S. (1994) Large scale mapping from small format imagery. *International Archives of Photogrammetry and Remote Sensing,* 30(4): 332-337.

Fraser, C. S. and Shortis, M. R. (1995) Metric exploitation of still video imagery. *Photogrammetric Record,* **15**(85): 107-122.

King, D. and Vlcek, J. (1990) Development of a multispectral video system and its application in forestry. *Canadian Journal of Remote Sensing,* **16**(1): 15-22.

King, D., Walsh, P. and Cuiffreda, F. (1994) Airborne digital frame camera imaging for elevation determination. *Photogrammetric Engineering and Remote Sensing,* **60**(11):1321-1326.

Louisse, C.J. and Van der Meulen, F. (1991) Future coastal defence in the Netherlands: strategies for protection and sustainable development. *Journal of Coastal Research,* **74**: 1027-1041.

Manzer, F.E. and Cooper, G.R. (1982) Use of portable video-taping for aerial infrared detection of potato disease. *Plant Disease,* **66**: 665-667.

Marsh, S., Walsh, J. and Sobrevila, C. (1994) Evaluation of airborne video data for landcover classification accuracy assessment in an isolated Brazilian forest. *Remote Sensing Environment,* **48**: 61-69.

Nixon, P., Escobar, D. and Menges, R. (1985) Use of a multiband video system for quick assessment of vegetal condition and discrimination of plant species. *Remote Sensing Environment,* **17**: 203-208.

Peipe, J. and Schneider, C.-T. (1995) High resolution still video camera for industrial photogrammetry. *Photogrammetric Record,* **15**(85): 135-139.

Use of NOAA/AVHRR Data in Desert Locust Control in the Algerian Sahara

R. Bonifacio[1] and A. Ouladichir[2]

[1]TAMSAT Group, Department of Meteorology, University of Reading, Reading RG6 2AU, UK.
[2]Organization Nationale de Meteorologie, D.R. Sud, BP I 1000 Tamanrasset, Algeria.

ABSTRACT

The low vegetation index levels associated with sparse vegetation in arid lands make changes in vegetation state susceptible to confusion, with variations in signal induced by soil, atmosphere and viewing geometry. The research presented in this paper used AVHRR data from a receiver sited at Tamanrasset in an attempt to improve the information for the reliable detection of sparse vegetation in arid lands for the monitoring of desert locust breeding areas. The NDVI (Normalized Difference Vegetation Index), SAVI (Soil Adjusted Vegetation Index), GEMI (Global Environment Monitoring Index) and PVI (Perpendicular Vegetation Index) were selected in order to assess their ability in separating the bare soil from the sparsely vegetated ground signal. A new approach using scene-based localized soil lines for the calculation of the PVI is presented. The PVI calculated in this way effectively removed soil primary and secondary effects, allowing the definition of a threshold for separating bare soil from vegetated ground which is applicable in both space and time. An operational programme for an Algerian remote sensing centre (CReVAM) to apply these findings is described. A case is made for the continued support of local remote sensing centres based on lessons learned from the satellite receiver's operation.

INTRODUCTION

A NOAA/AVHRR HRPT receiver was deployed in late 1991 at the Centre Regional de Veille Acrido Meteorologique (CReVAM) in Tamanrasset, southern Algeria, an institution dependent on the Algerian National Meteorological Office (ONM). The setting up and operation of the receiver was funded by the UK's Overseas Development Adminstration through the Natural Resources Institute (NRI) within the framework of its LARST programme (Local Application of Remote Sensing Techniques). Its main aim was to enhance the information available to local institutions (Plant Protection Services) for the monitoring of ecological conditions in the desert locust (*Schistocerca gregaria*) recession area.

In early 1993, it reached operational status, producing five NOAA channels for calibrated, co-registered image data, and products such as cloud and vegetation indices. The following years saw a steady improvement in the quality of the output, and this has been used as the focus for the ONM research programme for the desert regions. A network of automatic weather stations was deployed south of Tamanrasset, communication links were developed, and the Centre now has access to FTP/e-mail connections (*via* fax/telephone communication links) which it uses for updating NOAA orbital information. A monthly newsletter for the dissemination of information is now published, providing a description of the main weather events, a simple analysis of the synoptic situation, and rainfall data and vegetation indices time series for selected areas of interest. The present year saw a major update in the software.

One of the objectives of the project was to foster co-operation between the local institutions, specifically the Plant Protection Services (INPV) and the ONM. The INPV was seen as one of the main users of the satellite data; it was expected to use the information derived from vegetation indices to aid or even underpin survey and ground control measures against desert locusts. Co-operation was initially slow, partly because it was not the custom to collaborate with foreign organizations, but also because the INPV had no previous experience in the use of remotely sensed information and consequently needed good, sound arguments to incorporate it into their ground work. Recently, co-operation has been more forthcoming. The INPV has provided advice on the placement of the ONM automatic weather stations and currently, areas defined by the INPV are analysed in detail by the ONM team; results are published in the newsletter, which includes VI time series over the INPV survey areas and a summary of their species composition, degree of vegetation cover and soil wetness.

OPERATIONAL ACTIVITIES AND STUDY REGION CHARACTERISTICS

Until August 1995, the data processing of the operational work at the CReVAM consisted of:

- capture of a daily afternoon scene from the NOAA (11, then 14) satellite;
- processing with the BURS (Bradford University Research Systems) software to obtain five calibrated channels output, plus solar zenith and satellite view angle, in a lat/long grid, output in IDRISI format, for one region of interest;
- use of IDRISI routines to produce a cloud mask and to compute the several (cloud masked) vegetation indices under assessment;
- aggregation of results over a month for inclusion in the newsletter and for dissemination to the INPV.

The BURS software is only used for the production of five channels of remapped image data in a format suitable for a commercial (low-cost) GIS software package (IDRISI). All products are generated using IDRISI functions and run automatically (without operator intervention) using AWK programmes which generate BATCH programmes. They have been written as single keyword 'interfaces' which allow the user to carry out a desired sequence of operations from two or more pieces of commercial and specially written software that are repeated for operational work. These routines are simple to learn and provide the operator with intimate knowledge of the software and the machine being used. The data gathered during the 1992 and 1993 seasons allowed a description of the major features of the vegetation and rainfall regimes of the region.

Study Region and Data

The monitoring activities of the CReVAM focus on a region of Algeria south from 0.000° to 10.240° E and from 24.000° to 18.880° N (Figure 1). The dataset

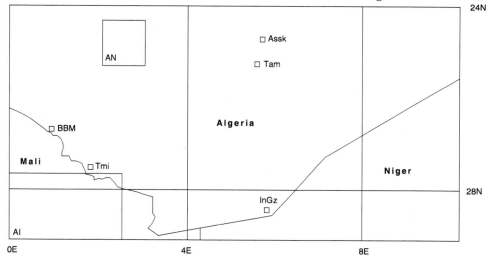

Figure 1. Map of the study area; rectangles AI and AN denote the sub-areas used in this study, AI = Adrar des Iforas, AN = Adrar Nahalet, squares indicate towns/ met. stations

consists of all five NOAA 11 channels, satellite view angle and solar zenith angle, and VIS (channel 1) and NIR (channel 2) top of the atmosphere reflectances (designated by R_1 and R_2, respectively); channels 3, 4 and 5 were obtained from the AVHRR raw data. The images were all co-registered to a set of topographical outlines but the absolute location was not verified. The data consisted of daily images for the 1993 season from mid-May to mid-November. In total, 35 images were available, seven in May, five in August, eight in September, 13 in October and five in November. Following preliminary inspection of the imagery, smaller areas where the strongest NDVI signal occurred were selected in the region of the Adrar des Iforas (Mali-Algeria border), extending from 0.060° to 2.560° E and 20.380° to 18.880° N, and in Adrar Nahalet (west of Tamanrasset) extending from 2.040° to 3.040° E and 22.70° to 23.70° N.

Vegetation and Rainfall

The rainfall network comprises five stations within the region, complemented by a set of automatic weather station in a denser arrangement south of the Hoggar mountains. Data from 6 years enable the characteristics of the region's rainfall regime to be outlined. The main rainy season is from June to August for the southern stations, but winter rains prevail for the northern stations. Sizeable single day amounts may fall at any time of the year, and low seasonal average totals range from 10 to 100 mm.

There can be very large daily falls; a single daily amount may constitute up to 75% of the seasonal total and a have very high spatial and temporal variability.

Prospects for rainfall estimation are not very high because of the small number of events gathered so far. Even with an acceptable rainfall estimation technique, the utility of rainfall information as a predictor of vegetation development is rather dubious, as rainfall is extensively redistributed by surface run-off.

Vegetation activity reaches a maximum between mid-September and early October, following the rains between June and August. Vegetation in these regions is confined to areas where the rainfall is concentrated along the drainage network. It is therefore more extensive in the *wadis* (dry river beds), which means that vegetation is arranged in linear features two or three HRPT (High Resolution Picture Transmission) pixels wide at the most. Significant increases in vegetation index values, indicating the start of a 'green-growth' period, usually occur in August and September. Within the areas of marked seasonal vegetation growth (e.g. area AI in Figure 1), noticeable and consistent differences in the date of the 'greening-up' are observed, reaching 20–30 days between points 1° of longitude apart. This is linked to the topography and geology of the region which determines the redistribution of rainfall over a wider area.

Problems of Monitoring Work

Routine operational work at the CReVAM uses the NDVI as a monitoring tool. The main problems associated with its use are as follows.

1. Strong viewing geometry-induced variations can be an important fraction of the total seasonal variation. NDVI of low vegetation levels during the wet season are confused with bare soil NDVI values from early on in the season (due to reduced atmospheric water vapour amounts), and this causes problems in the interpretation of NDVI time series.

2. Soils in the region reach NDVI values well within the range of vegetation values (e.g. 0.15).

On the positive side, vegetation causes a well-defined response in channel 3 (mid-infrared, 3.7 gm), lowering the brightness temperature relative to the bare soil values (the same can be observed in channels 4 and 5, though the effect is less pronounced). Also, in channel 1 (VIS) a decrease in reflectance values relative to the bare soil values is evident. These vegetation features are used to help discriminate vegetation from soil at the lower end of the NDVI signal or in case of a bare soil, high NDVI effect, but this has to be done in an interactive way by the observers. Additionally, vegetation grows over very bright soils so the resulting NDVI values are not very susceptible to aerosol interference (Tanre et al., 1992). The small values of atmospheric water vapour on most days, coupled with the high frequency of clear sky views, lead to a reduced (though not insignificant) importance of the atmospheric interference. The short-term fluctuations this induces in vegetation index values are well accounted for by 5-day or weekly maximum value compositing. Of greater influence are the low frequency variations in atmospheric humidity from the dry (April-May) to the wet season (July-October), due to the seasonal northwards movement of moist air masses responsible for problem 2 above.

ALTERNATIVE VEGETATION INDICES

The use of vegetation indices for monitoring vegetation conditions is a routine application of NOAA/AVHRR data (Prince and Justice, 1991). The high temporal frequency of observation, and the wide areal coverage of these data, makes them prime tools for monitoring efforts in data-sparse regions with difficult access such as the Algerian Sahara. However, the reliability, behaviour and interpretation of the variety of vegetation indices so far developed is largely unknown for the sparse vegetation in arid lands. This work attempted to provide some insight into the abilities of different vegetation indices to discriminate vegetation from bare soil in arid conditions.

A variety of vegetation indices has been investigated with the objective of removing or minimizing the problems outlined above. Those which will be analysed are the NDVI (Tucker, 1979) as the most widely used/researched, the SAVI (Huete, 1988) supposed to minimize bare soil variability, the GEMI (Pinty and Verstraete, 1992) supposed to be less susceptible to atmospheric interference, and the PVI (Richardson and Wiegand, 1977) which incorporates soil spectral reflectance behaviour (the soil line) in its formulation.

$$NDVI = (R_2 - R_1)/(R_2 + R_1) \tag{1}$$

$$SAVI = (I + L)(R_2 - R_1)/(R_2 + R_1 + L), \text{ with } L=0 \tag{2}$$

$$GEMI = \eta.(1 - 0.25.\eta) - (R_1 - 0.125)/(1 - R_1) \tag{3a}$$

$$\text{where } \eta = 2.(R_2^2 (R_1^2) + 1.5R_2 + 0.5R_1 / (R_2 + R_1 + 0.5) \tag{3b}$$

$$PVI = (R_2 - a.R_1 - b) / (a^2 + 1)_{1/2} \tag{4}$$

where a, b are the soil line slope and intercept, i.e., R_2.soil = a.R_1soil + b

R_1, R_2 = AVHRR channel 1,2

The first three indices are calculated directly from R_1 and R_2 values. The PVI, however, requires the prior calculation of the soil line coefficients. Details on the background and derivation of these and other vegetation indices can be found in Baret and Guyot (1991). The PVI includes some information on the soil reflectance characteristics, but the way in which this information is included is very important. Although the concept of a soil line is a simple one, its application over large areas with a wide variety of soil and surface types may be problematic. Ideally, a soil line should be calculated over areas of the same soil but this would require information which is not usually available. The alternative approach is to calculate a single global soil line for the whole scene under analysis, thus combining a large number of different soils, but this would defeat the purpose of minimizing bare soil variability. The approach chosen here attempts to localize the soil lines by calculating them over small areas. Pixel R_1 and R_2 values over a square of N x N pixels are extracted and correlated, and the slope, intercept and coefficient of correlation obtained are assigned to the central pixel of the N x N square. The process is repeated by 'sliding' this square along the image and the end results are images of slope (a), intercept (b) and correlation coefficient (r). Values of these three parameters for a given pixel describe the soil line for the N x N pixels around it. The choice of N is a compromise between having enough pixels for a meaningful correlation, and not including too many different soils within the same soil line. A value of N–9 was chosen for the subsequent analysis. Further details can be found in Bonifacio *et al.* (1995).

A COMPARISON OF VEGETATION INDICES

Evaluation
The main aim of this study was to reduce the bare soil variability to a minimum so that a characteristic threshold separating soil from vegetation could be specified. Variations in vegetation index values within a period of unmistakable vegetation growth are deemed less important for the monitoring efforts at this stage (though they may be of some value in discrimination of different vegetation communities). The NDVI, SAVI and GEMI were obtained from R_1 and R_2 images according to equations (1), (2) and (3). The PVI is formulated from the images of soil line slope and coefficient according to (4). For some of these comparisons, soil line slope and intercept were also calculated for the whole scene under analysis, and a resulting PVI was calculated. This was designated PVIG (global PVI) as opposed to PVIL (local PVI), the PVI calculated from the local soil lines.

In order to analyse the effectiveness of the different indices in the removal of soil effects, data from the region of the Adrar Nahalet were chosen as they illustrate a common problem of desert regions, bare soils with high NDVI values. Here, the NDVI reaches values of 0.15 (with even higher values observed in past seasons) even though it was confirmed that the area was devoid of vegetation from ground verification and examination of the individual channel data (absence of R_1 values lower than surroundings, accompanied by saturation of channels 3, 4 and 5).

Figure 2a shows the NDVI, SAVI and GEMI profiles along a transect through a soil effect area. The values of these three indices are well within the typical range of values of vegetation. Results for the PVI are shown in Figure 2b. It can be seen that the behaviour of the PVI depends crucially on the definition of the soil line; the PVIG values show the same overlap into the vegetated range of values as the NDVI, SAVI and GEMI, and the spatial pattern of the PVIG corresponds to that of the NDVI and SAVI. However, the PVIL shows a much reduced variation along the same transect, with values reaching a maximum of 0.007 (below the typical sparsely vegetated values above 0.01) but mostly varying around 0. The spatial pattern of the PVIL image is nearly uniform with noise-like small variations. This shows that the PVI calculated from local soil lines is able to reduce the bare soil variability to a maximum.

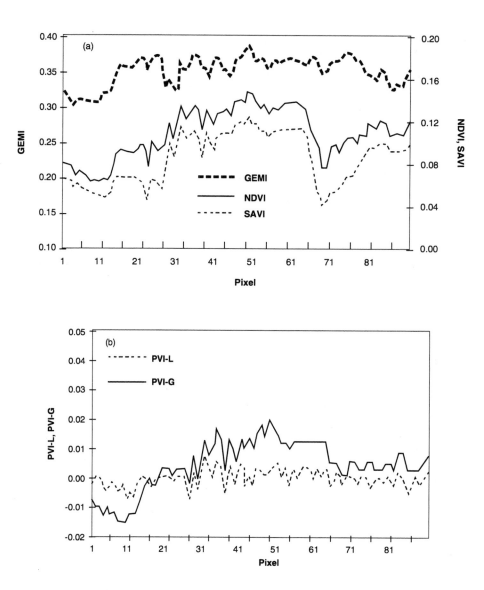

Figure 2. Vegetation index values along a bare soil transect in the Adrar Nahalet region. (a) NDVI, SAVI and GEMI: note high values of all three indices between pixels 30 to 60. (b) PVIL (calculated from localized soil lines) and PVIG (calculated from a single image wide soil line): note that the soil artifact is still present in the PVIG but not in PVIL.

The above problem is relevant for the analysis of a single scene. The other way in which the bare soil signal may cause problems in the interpretation of vegetation index data is in the analysis of time series over sparsely vegetated areas with a well-defined dry and wet season, as is the case within the Sahel/Sahara transition (roughly the latitude band 16° to 22°N). The NDVI (and other indices) values for the dry season (from bare soil) overlap the values for the wet season (from vegetation) because of reduced atmospheric interference in the dry season (drier atmosphere).

In order to evaluate the abilities of the PVIL to resolve these seasonal ambiguities, time sequences of all vegetation indices were examined. A representative example is shown for the PVI and the NDVI (the other two indices gave very much the same picture as the NDVI) in Figure 3. These provide clear evidence that the local PVI (PVIL) does separate the early season bare soil signal from the sparse vegetation signal under increased atmospheric

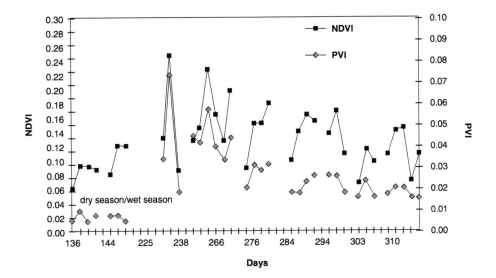

Figure 3. Time series of daily NDVI and PVI values for a vegetated area in the Adrar des Iforas region. Note how the dry season PVI values are clearly separated from the wet season ones even in the case of marked atmospheric interference. The NDVI (and also the SAVI and GEMI) values during the dry season do not offer this clear separation. Compositing the NDVI values does not always provide a solution to the problem.

interference. The PVI is less sensitive to the effect of low frequency atmospheric interference than other indices. The local PVI threshold value for bare soil based on the satellite data seems to be 0.01. This threshold applies over a wide region and throughout the season, unlike other vegetation indices for which there is no well-defined bare soil threshold, i.e., bare soil NDVI threshold values change over a region or in time for the same location. Even for composited time series, the identification of the moment when the vegetation index shows an upward trend was seen to be much clearer with the local PVI than with any other index.

Figure 3 also shows the behaviour of the PVI and NDVI over vegetated areas. The general behaviour of all indices was very similar, though there were some differences in the detail which will have to wait for a more detailed analysis (and a more extensive dataset) before they can be resolved.

Conclusions
The interpretation of vegetation index data in arid regions is fraught with difficulties. There are problems of confusion over bare soil signals within the same image (due to soil spectral reflectance characteristics) and for the same location over the course of the season (due to changes in atmospheric composition). The most prominent vegetation indices (NDVI, SAVI, GEMI and PVI) were evaluated for their ability to minimize these problems. A new method for the quantification of the bare soil spectral reflectance characteristics is proposed and incorporated into the calculation of the PVI. It is shown that the PVI computed in this way effectively removes the bare soil and low frequency atmospheric effects and is able to isolate the vegetation signal. Based on these preliminary results, a PVI threshold of 0.01 provides a soil/vegetation threshold value which is applicable across a wide geographical area and throughout the whole season.

These first results raise a number of questions which will be the object of the research plan, outlined below, to be carried out mainly by staff of the CReVAM using the data from NOAA-14 over the next few seasons:

1. evaluate and analyse the short-term and long-term variations in the soil line coefficients and relate them to factors such as atmospheric conditions and viewing geometry variations;
2. evaluate a larger group of vegetation indices and carry out field verification of vegetation cover to check against their values; and
3. analyse the seasonal trends of the vegetation indices.

It should be noted that at this stage, the use of the PVI as defined here seems only applicable to areas where vegetation has similar spatial distribution characteristics, i.e., where vegetated pixels fill only part of the N x N chosen to calculate the soil line (desert or transition to desert areas). In areas where extensive vegetation is present all year round, this method is not applicable, and in areas with large seasonal fluctuations from bare ground to full vegetation cover, it is probably only applicable during the dry season. In any case, for vegetated ground the behaviour of all indices is very similar, hence there is little to be gained by using the PVI. Even if this proves to be a method of strictly local application, it fulfills the main duty of a local remote sensing centre which is to meet the information requirements of local users.

FUTURE PERSPECTIVES AND APPRAISAL OF EXPERIENCE

Future Plans

The changes brought about by the extensive software update have generated a more ambitious plan for the next and following seasons, although the basic data processing design outlined above is retained.

1. The operational area of capture is to be enlarged to 1536 x 1536 pixels, 15°N to 25°S, 10° longitude wide, varying within 15°W to 25°E limits.
2. The list of INPV survey areas is to be digitized for time series extraction. The daily loop of METEOSAT TIR (Thermal InfraRed) data will be used to monitor occurrence of large storm clouds over desert areas with follow-up by AVHRR in the following days. In this way, a proper monitoring mode will be installed at the centre. These rainfall events comprise most or all of the seasonal amount, so early warning if they hit population centres may be very positive. The possibly vegetated ground afterwards may provide breeding ground for locusts and the data gathered may prove useful for research products.
3. The list of products is to be enlarged with indices of atmospheric interference. The cloud mask $(R_1/Tb5)$ is to be perfected with seasonal and maybe spatial dependence. The other empirical atmospheric indices are the Tb4-Tb5 difference and a reflectance contrast function. Local operators will analyse variation of these with view angle, time of season and occurrence of cloud, as they will provide useful information for the interpretation of vegetation index single date and composited imagery.
4. Vegetation index evaluation will continue but the newsletter will probably focus only on NDVI and local PVI results. The suitability of the INPV ground data in the evaluation of vegetation indices will be verified.
5. Rainfall data will be collected into spreadsheets to relate to METEOSAT CCD amounts. This will use all available data, but may need to wait before enough data accumulates.

Learning from Experience

It is believed that the above project provides a good example of the potential of a small remote sensing meteorological centre. Can any useful lessons be learned from the problems it has faced and the experience gained? The most desirable consequence of the investment made in such a centre would be to have an independent research and operational institution supported by its own government and able to make progress either independently, or spurred by suggestions from other (foreign) institutions. This is too ambitious as a practical aim but some progress can be made through the way in which the processing software works, the way the installation of a receiver is planned, and the way the long-term relationship is organized.

Software

The versions of the processing software from BURS proved to be reliable tools and simple and quick to use (once specifically tailored). However, it should be noted that the processing is done only up to the production of calibrated, co-located and re-projected data in an easy to handle lat/long grid. All the products and subsequent data extracted use a commercial low-cost GIS software package (IDRISI). This was initially to overcome the difficulties posed by the nature of the environment being studied and the lack of facilities such as cloud masking or alternative vegetation indices. There was also a need to use local specifics (e.g. dark mountains against sandy soils instead of coastlines for co-location and atmospheric contrast). If local institutions are to carry out research, they should be given software which is amenable to adaptation and customization so that it can incorporate operational versions of their own or other people's research efforts. The BURS software provides this facility, and it is hoped that the current Windows version of the NOAA Operational Manager will retain it. This feature of the processing software may not be available in the future, but if the new software version provides output in an easily used alternative format(s) which allows for adaptation and customizing, problems should not arise.

Training Programs

Catering for local needs or taking advantage of local specifics implies that the installation of the receiver should be accompanied by a user training programme with a focus on the science behind the application and acquisition of remotely sensed data. Users can then effectively build bespoke systems tailored to their needs using remote sensing as a tool.

Long-term Support

Providing for long-term support is deemed essential for the success of the local centres. At the lowest level, it consists simply of updating the software with more modern versions and providing fixes for bugs. This task may not be trivial if there are operating system transitions to be made (e.g. DOS to Windows). Provision of hardware depends on the money involved but should cover low-cost components. There are immediate benefits to be derived as the local centre provides the ultimate testing ground for new versions of software. Long-term support becomes easier if the output from the centres is used in research efforts abroad, but even if this is not the case, some degree of scientific and programming support should be provided. Accumulated experience should eventually ease the demands.

REFERENCES

Baret, F. and Guyot, G. (1991) Potential and limits of vegetation indices for LAI and APAR assessment. *Remote Sensing of the Environment,* **35**: 161-173.

Bonifacio, R., Milford, J.R., Dugdale, G., Ouladichir, A. (1995) Detection of sparse vegetation in the Sahara Desert with NOAA/AVHRR data. *Proceedings of the Meteorological Satellite User's Conference (Polar Orbiting Systems), Winchester, September 1995.*

Huete, A.R. (1988) A soil adjusted vegetation index (SAVI). *Remote Sensing of the Environment,* **19**: 295-309.

Pinty, B. and Verstraete, M.M. (1992) GEMI : a non-linear index to monitor global vegetation from satellites. *Vegetatio,* **101**: 15-20.

Prince, S.D. and Justice, C.O. (1991) Editorial. *International Journal of Remote Sensing*, **12**(6): 1137-1146.

Richardson, A.J. and Wiegand, C.L. (1977) Distinguishing vegetation from soil background information. *Photogrammetry Engineering and Remote Sensing*, **43**: 1541-1552.

Tanre, D., Holben B.N. and Kaufman, Y.J. (1992) Atmospheric correction algorithm for NOAA-AVHRR products: theory and application, I.E.E.E. *Transactions in Geoscience and Remote Sensing*, **GE-30**(2): 231-248.

Tucker, C.J. (1979) Red and infrared linear combinations for monitoring vegetation. *Remote Sensing of the Environment*, **8**: 127-150.

Use of GIS to Assist Hydrological Modelling of Lake Basins in the Kenya Rift Valley — Conclusions

M. J. Stuttard[1], J. B. Hayball[1], G. Narciso[2], M. Suppo[2], A. Oroda[3] and J. Baraza[3]

[1]Earth Observation Sciences Ltd, Farnham Business Park, Weydon Lane, Farnham, Surrey, UK.
[2]Aquater SpA, CP 20-61047, San Lorenzo in Campo, (PS), Italy.
[3]Regional Centre for Services in Surveying Mapping and Remote Sensing, PO Box 18118, Nairobi, Kenya.

ABSTRACT

This paper reports the final results of an EC supported (STD-3) project which integrated satellite and ground data in a GIS to model water level changes on three closed lakes in the Central Kenyan Rift Valley. These lakes (Nakuru, Naivasha, Elementeita) are economically and ecologically valuable but are subject to changing water levels. The degree to which human activities such as water abstraction and land use change affected lake level was not previously known. The model developed during the project attempted to answer such questions. Landsat TM and MSS imagery were used to create a land use map as input to the model, and a time series of NOAA AVHRR data assisted in the estimation of evapotranspiration. Monthly rainfall data from 53 rain gauges were collated for a nine year period. The model used land reference units created by GIS overlay of soils, topography, land use and other data. It was run on a monthly basis over nine years for each of the lake catchments, providing change in lake level as the output. The effect on lake level was shown for two scenarios, construction of a reservoir and water diversion outside the catchment.

INTRODUCTION

The project from which this work arose was funded under the EC STD-3 Programme on Life Sciences and Technologies for Developing Countries. The primary objective was to create a GIS database and use it to implement a hydrological model capable of accurately simulating lake level changes for lakes Naivasha, Nakuru and Elementeita in the Kenyan Rift Valley. Vital considerations were that the method developed should be transferable to other lake basins, should use relatively simple data, and should incorporate the effect of management practices.

Lakes Naivasha, Nakuru and Elementeita are the most elevated and centrally located members of a chain of lakes within the eastern branch of the Great African Rift Valley. The three lake catchments are enclosed by an area of 90 x 90 km, located between latitudes 0°15' and 0°30' S, and longitudes 36°0' and 36°30' E. This area is 70 km northwest of Nairobi and is confined by the Nyandarua Mountains to the east (exceeding 3960 m) and the Mau Escarpment to the west (exceeding 3000 m). The valley width here is between 45 and 70 km.

The lakes lie in the broad, level floor of the rift at an elevation of about 1800 m (1200–2000m below the escarpments). Approximate surface areas of the lakes are: Naivasha, 133 km^2; Nakuru, 45 km^2; and Elementeita, 22 km^2. Nakuru and Elementeita are closed alkaline (soda) lakes, with no significant outflows. It is suggested (Melack, 1988; Vareschi, 1982) that the levels of these two lakes are a direct response to the balance of rainfall and evaporation. Between 1958 and 1974, the depth of Elementeita fluctuated between 0.3 m and 3.1 m. Regular measurements on Naivasha were started in 1908 and since then, the lake level has varied by 9 m, the overall trend being a reduction in level (Harper et al., 1990).

Wildlife, especially the huge flocks of flamingos on Elementeita and Nakuru, generates significant tourist revenue and the fresh water of Naivasha supports fisheries as well as high value irrigated horticulture and agriculture; changes in lake level are thus intimately linked with both ecology and economy.

While lake levels have fluctuated quite naturally since prehistoric times as a result of climatic changes, there is concern that recent trends are directly influenced by accelerating land use change and water demands in the area. In order to assess the potential impact of further environmental changes on lake level, it is necessary to have a reliable model. Therefore, the primary aim of the work was to implement a hydrological model capable of accurately simulating lake level changes on a monthly basis, taking into account human influences. In order to calibrate and validate the model, a time series of data was assembled for 108 months between January 1985 and December 1993.

The approach is based on the concept of land reference units (LRUs), each unit having a unique set of parameters (e.g. area, slope, permeability) defining its hydrology. Additionally, dynamic data inputs, i.e., rainfall, number of rain days and actual evapotranspiration (AET), are represented by their contribution to the water flow within these LRUs on a monthly basis over the study period.

HYDROLOGICAL MODEL

The hydrological model simulates the total discharge to the lake on a monthly basis. In addition, by integrating river catchments into the spatial data sets, the model is able to simulate the monthly discharge of individual rivers.

The model contains two elements: first, a set of general mathematical equations describes different hydrological regimes which may exist in a catchment; second, a detailed analysis of the lake basin determines which physical, meteorological and geographic parameters can be used to distinguish between regions falling under different hydrological regimes. The latter process is termed 'on-line conceptualization'.

The model was designed to operate on spatial data units, enabling it to simulate changes in the spatial datasets such as a change of land use within the catchment. This makes it very much more useful for water resource modelling than a simple lake water balance model and avoids the complexity of a fully distributed model (i.e., one which attempts to describe the complete hydrological system).

LRUs were defined by variables identified in the detailed on-line conceptualization. Therefore, the LRU map contains regions for which a homogeneous hydrological regime can be said to exist. This allows each LRU to be treated as a single entity. Thus, a simple hydrological system can be simulated in each month, in that unit, using a single set of static variables (such as soil class, slope, land use, etc.) and dynamic inputs (e.g. rainfall, evapotranspiration, etc.). In this way, the contribution of water from each LRU to the lake can be calculated on a monthly basis. The monthly change in lake water storage was converted to a change in lake level using a volume/depth relationship derived from bathymetric charts.

LINKING THE MODEL AND GIS

Once the model was stated mathematically, it was possible to identify all those elements which have a spatial expression. The LRU is the key to the interface between the spatial/geometric information contained in the GIS and the tabular inputs to the hydrological model. It allows the model to treat each LRU as a discrete entity, with a single hydrological regime applied to a set of static and dynamic inputs. As the LRUs are hydrologically homogeneous, they can be represented as records in a table.

DATA COLLECTION AND INTEGRATION

The model was strongly influenced by the need to work with relatively simple data. Existing topographic maps of Kenya were good, so these were vector-digitized to obtain catchment boundaries, lake shoreline and contours. A digital elevation model was generated from the digitized contours and a slope map was derived from this. Available water capacity was estimated from the exploratory soil map of Kenya using soil depth and texture.

Data for rainfall and rain days were obtained from a mixture of daily records on disk and monthly paper records. Spreadsheet software was ideal for integrating the data. Eventually, monthly datasets were assembled for 53 rain gauges over the 108 month period, but 14% of rainfall, and 11% of rain days figures were missing. Missing rainfall data were reconstructed using a separate stepwise multiple regression model for each month. Interestingly, the regression approach was found to provide a better estimate at a missing data point than a spatial interpolation because of the high spatial variability of rainfall in the project area.

A somewhat crude land use map was derived using geometrically rectified satellite images (Landsat MSS (1976) and TM (1989)) covering the study area. Supervised classification was carried out with image processing software using ground data collected from field survey. A thematic map containing 10 spectrally distinct classes was produced. This was then simplified to 5 classes (Forest, Pasture, Agriculture, Urban, Water) by merging classes from the more detailed map. Both maps were easily transferred to the GIS from the image processing software.

The most problematic dataset to assemble was that for the components of actual evapotranspiration (AET). AET can be calculated as open water evaporation multiplied by a transpiration coefficient. On a monthly time base, the transpiration coefficient is determined by energy balance; thus, it was estimated from the albedo (Bøgh and Søgaard, 1993). Open water evaporation was estimated for the rainfall stations and the transpiration coefficient was based on the albedo of different land use classes. Firstly, monthly evaporation was obtained from pan evaporimeter measurements available from four meteorological stations in or near the area. This dataset was spatially re-distributed over 53 rain gauge sites using cluster analysis to assign each gauge to the most similar meteorological station. Secondly, albedo estimates were obtained, on an average monthly basis, using a time series of images from the AVHRR sensor on the NOAA-11 satellite (Saunders, 1990). The albedo maps were combined with the land use map to obtain average monthly albedo per land use class.

All these datasets were stored as a combination of maps and associated attribute tables in the GIS.

SPATIAL ANALYSIS

Having constructed the dataset, a series of spatial analysis operations was used to create the set of tables for input to the model.

Creation of the LRU Map
The LRU map was made by overlaying separate maps of lake basin, river section, rain gauge site, Voronoi class (i.e., Thiessen polygon), land use class,

altitude switch, soil class and lake identity. Special effort was required to ensure that common boundaries in the different maps were identical so that slivers (spurious new regions) were minimized. This overlay operation produced a map of unique combinations arising from the union of classes on the input maps, and it was further processed so that each topologically distinct region had a unique identifier. In order to eliminate very small regions, a 3 x 3 modal filter was applied, resulting in a final set of 8310 LRUs.

Addition of Static Data to LRU Attributes

Having created the map and calculated the area of each LRU, the LRU centroids were used to extract class codes from the source maps (lake basins, river section sub-catchments, soils, Voronoi, land use) and append them as new fields in the LRU attribute table. For example, a 'rainfall peak' switch was flagged as 'on' if the average August rainfall in an LRU exceeded both the July and September figures by a factor greater than 1.2. This required only a simple operation on the table of long-term average rainfall.

Calculating Rainfall for Each LRU

To calculate rainfall in each LRU for all 108 months, each month of rainfall data was interpolated as a continuous surface from the rain gauge (point) data, then an area weighted average was computed for each LRU using the GIS.

Following a comparative trial of interpolation accuracy and efficiency for four different methods of rainfall interpolation (Thiessen, linear, non-linear and distance decay), the linear interpolation method was selected as it provided a stable surface which passed through the available data points with good interpolation accuracy.

Calculating Rain Days for Each LRU

The nature of the rain days data is such that any form of weighted interpolation is not physically realistic because in this area, there is little correlation between the number of rain days at any given site and the sites closest to it. Therefore, a spatial estimation of rain days was obtained using the Voronoi map derived from the locations of the rain gauge sites. All LRUs falling within a particular Voronoi polygon were assigned the same number of monthly raindays as occurred at the gauge located within the polygon.

As the Voronoi map was used as one input to the LRU map, each LRU fell entirely within just one Voronoi polygon. Hence, the rain days value for each LRU could be looked up in the associated rain gauge data table.

Determining AET for Each LRU

Evaporation on each LRU was obtained from a relational look-up table of monthly evaporation values for the meteorological station associated with the rain gauge site corresponding to the Voronoi class of the LRU. The albedo value was found by a look-up in the table of albedo values for the month of the year and the land use class of the LRU. Using these values, monthly AET was calculated for each LRU in the study area.

Determining Volume/Depth Relationship for Lakes

The GIS was also used to obtain the lake volume/depth relationship from a gridded bathymetric model.

CALIBRATION AND VALIDATION

Calibration and validation were carried out on separate periods of the time series.

The calibration procedure was split into two phases. In the first phase, all the aspects relating to climatic, morphological and hydrogeological characteristics of the system were examined, and probable ranges for the coefficients were established. Using these ranges as a basis, a trial and error procedure was adopted to assign exact values to the model's coefficients. This involved varying a single coefficient within its assumed range while holding all other coefficients constant. The results of the simulations were then compared with the measured lake levels over the calibration period, and various goodness-of-fit indicators were calculated to establish the optimum value.

In the validation phase, an analysis of many simulations was made in order to characterize the operation of the model. Comparisons were made between simulated and recorded values for the levels of all three lakes, and the discharge at five river gauging stations. Additionally, an analysis of the sensitivity of the model to various input parameters was made. Perturbations to the rainfall, AET, AWC data and land use classes were made and the model re-run with the new data. The results were compared with the same simulation using unperturbed data and this indicated that the model was robust for a range of conditions.

RESULTS

The results of the simulation are shown below for Lake Naivasha, together with the recorded lake level data (Figure 1).

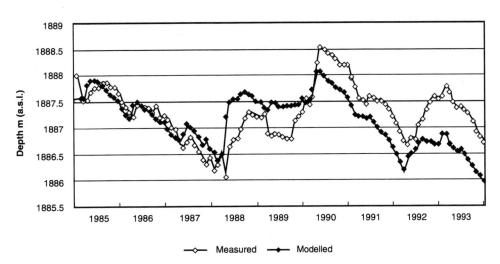

Figure 1. Results of simulation for Lake Naivasha

It can be seen that with a few notable exceptions, monthly changes in lake level are modelled with a reasonable degree of accuracy. The error in conservation of water volume over the entire validation period was 8% which compares favourably with the general performance of hydrological models. The errors introduced in each estimation of lake volume change accumulate over time and hence, the simulated and recorded data tend to diverge. As the model was not intended to be a precise predictive tool but was designed to aid water resource management in the catchment, the accumulation of errors is acceptable because, although it is not absolutely accurate, it is still physically realistic. The model can therefore be used to make comparisons between successive simulations under different catchment conditions.

USING THE MODEL

Management decisions concerning water resources and land use are widely assumed to have an impact on the overall discharge of the basin, thus influencing to a certain extent, the level of water in the lakes. The model developed in this project can be applied to the study of these interactions. Land and water use practices can potentially affect all aspects of hydrological and ecological systems, and an integrated use of GIS and modelling facilities can effectively simulate new 'scenarios'.

The first scenario considered was a hypothetical water diversion from one of the rivers feeding Naivasha. A water diversion scheme which takes water out of the catchment for the supply of Nakuru and Gilgil towns has in fact been implemented in the Naivasha catchment. The scenario presented in Figure 2 below does not attempt to reproduce this controversial scheme accurately, though the abstraction rates are comparable. A variable monthly release rate was simulated with reference to the Malewa River. The amount was a monthly 20% diversion reduced by 0.03 million m^3 (roughly corresponding to the minimum flow in the analysed period) in order to guarantee a constant free water flow into the river section.

In a second scenario, a hypothetical reservoir was created and regulated so that the residual discharge into the river was lower than the natural one during the

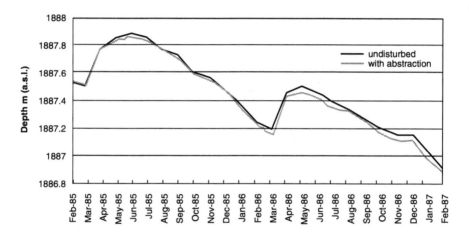

Figure 2. 'Scenario' simulated by integrated use of GIS and modelling facilities

wet season but generally higher in the dry season. The overall effect of the reservoir was a relative reduction in lake level (within a range of 2–14 cm) which still followed the undisturbed pattern of fluctuation.

With reference to these results, it is possible to decide whether the calculated decrease of the water level is significant with respect to the natural environment or the economy of the surrounding agricultural areas, for example.

CONCLUSION

The technical outputs of this project, comprising an environmental information system and a specially designed hydrological model structure, form a powerful management tool to support the development of water and land management policies.

Although many other institutional and political factors may govern major decisions on watershed management, decision makers can use this type of information as an 'objective' analysis element in the framework of sustainable socio-economic and environmental development.

The basic environmental data which have been integrated into a homogeneous and accessible form, also have great potential for a wider range of applications in the project area. These include land use planning, wildlife and vegetation studies and wetland conservation planning.

None of the individual components are new in terms of science, but the project has demonstrated how an integrated technical approach embracing a relatively simple physical model, GIS and remote sensing techniques, can result in a potentially effective decision support tool.

REFERENCES

Bøgh, E. and Søgaard, H. (1993) Interaction between landforms, vegetation and waterbalance in the Sahel studied by use of GIS, satellite images and data from HAPEX-Sahel. pp. 73-90. In: *Proceedings from the Seminar on Satellite Remote Sensing in Developing Countries, Institute of Geography, University of Copenhagen, 24-25 May 1993.*

Harper, D.M., Mavuti, K.M. and Muchiri, S.M. (1990) Ecology and management of Lake Naivasha, Kenya, in relation to climatic change, alien species' introductions, and agricultural development. *Environmental Conservation,* 17: 328-336.

Melack, J.M. (1988) Primary producer dynamics associated with evaporative concentration in a shallow, equatorial soda lake (Lake Elementeita, Kenya). *Hydrobiologia,* 158: 1-14.

Saunders, R.W. (1990) The determination of broad surface albedo from AVHRR visible and near infrared radiances. *International Journal of Remote Sensing,* 11: 741-752.

Vareschi, E. (1982) The ecology of Lake Nakuru (Kenya). III. Abiotic factors and primary production. *Oecologia,* 55: 81-101.

Environmental Impact Assessment of Tsetse Control: Historical Quantification of Land Cover and Land Use

Alan Mills and Judith Pender

Natural Resources Institute, Central Avenue, Chatham Maritime, Chatham, Kent, ME4 4TB, UK.

ABSTRACT

Tsetse flies are a major constraint to livestock production in tropical Africa through their transmission of animal trypanosomiasis. Control of tsetse has been the primary method of reducing trypanosomiasis in Zimbabwe for more than 50 years, and in northwestern Zimbabwe near Lake Kariba, the limit of fly distribution has been pushed northwards since 1980 by successive campaigns using a variety of control methods. The effect of tsetse control on land use and natural vegetation has been investigated over a 20-year period. Remotely sensed data have proved useful in identifying land cover and quantifying change in an area where there is little information from other sources. Landsat Thematic Mapper (TM) data were used to identify 15 land cover classes, including one representing land use dominated by humans. Land use changes from 1972 to 1993 were quantified using Landsat TM and Multi-Spectral Scanner (MSS) data. The results of these measurements from the Kariyangwe area in Manjolo Communal Land are presented in this paper. The pattern of land use change is complex, involving intensification in already settled areas, expansion to virgin land, and occasional contraction. Expansion into preferred vegetation complexes can be seen. There is a wide range of factors affecting patterns of land use change, and a small sub-set of variables studied here demonstrates the potential for using remotely sensed data with other datasets in a GIS to interpret land use change.

INTRODUCTION

Bovine trypanosomiasis transmitted by tsetse fly (*Glossina* spp.) has long been recognized as a major constraint to rural development and livestock production in Zimbabwe. Areas below 1070 m are climatically suitable for tsetse, and approximately half the country has a long history of infestation (Lovemore, 1994). Since the late 19th century, successive Zimbabwean governments have attempted to control tsetse by various means. Insecticide spraying started in 1953 and continued until operations were curtailed by the Independence War of the late 1970s; this resulted in substantial re-infestation. Large-scale control efforts were resumed in 1982 (Hursey and Allsopp, 1983), so tsetse are now largely confined to the Zambesi Valley and the northern border with Mozambique.

There is a growing awareness of the importance of supporting the implementation of tsetse control programmes with resource and economic data on potential land use changes in areas which have been opened up to livestock and settlement (Prankherd, 1991). This paper presents some of the results of a study to assess the effects of tsetse clearance on land cover in an area bordering Lake Kariba, by quantifying spatial and temporal changes in human dominated land use over a 20-year period in relation to natural vegetation, geology, the road network and tsetse control history.

The Study Area

The study area covers 8478 km² bordering Lake Kariba between Mlibizi at 18°10'S and Bumi Hills at 16°50' S (Figure 1). The climate is semi-arid with dry land farming practised in the three Communal Areas of Manjolo, Siabuwa and Omay. The study area also includes the Chizarira National Park, Chete Safari Area, Sijarira Forest, and three small areas of state land at Mlibizi, Binga and Bumi Hills. This paper will concentrate on an examination of one part of the study area, Kariyangwe, in the southeastern part of Manjolo Communal Land (Figure 1).

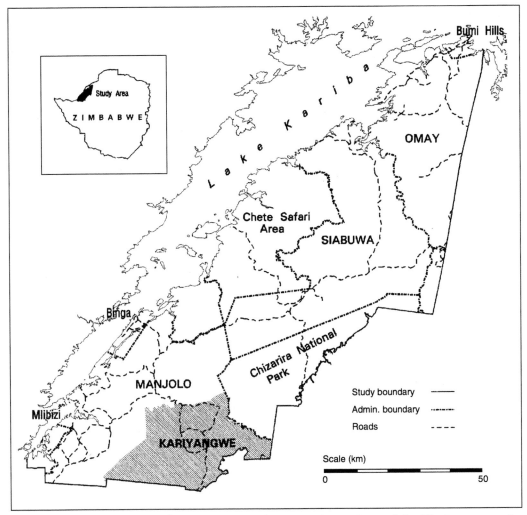

Figure 1. The study area showing major administrative units and the Kariyangwe sub-region

The Kariyangwe study area, covering 1678 km², comprises a basin in the middle reaches of the Sebungwe River, and the surrounding hills. The main area of settlement is almost completely surrounded by low escarpments which, until recently, confined settlement to the basin (Figure 2). The geology of the basin is characterized by glacial deposits dating from the Permian (Karoo) surrounded by Triassic (Karoo) grits, sandstones and siltstones to the southwest, and Late Precambrian red grits, sandstones, shales and conglomerates to the north and east above the escarpments (Figure 3). In the northwest, there is an area of gneiss of unknown geologic age. The three main watercourses running through the area join to form the Sebungwe River which drains through a narrow gorge to Lake Kariba (Figure 2).

Natural vegetation is mainly single dominance *Colophospermum mopane* woodland although in the northeast, complexes of *Julbernadia globiflora* dominated woodland (including miombo woodlands of *Julbernadia* sp. and *Brachestygia* spp. on steep slopes) occur; *Combretum* spp. woodland is found to the west. Much of the woodland beyond the basin has mixed species including *Brachestygia* spp., *Kirkia acuminiata*, *Terminalia prunioides* and *Strychos madagascariensis*.

Kariyangwe was part of a series of tsetse control campaigns during the 1970s and early 1980s (Douthwaite and Tingle, 1994; Lovemore, 1994) and was infested with tsetse up to 1986. Operations between 1978 and independence in 1980 were limited by a deteriorating security situation, but they were resumed from 1981 onwards (Lovemore, 1994).

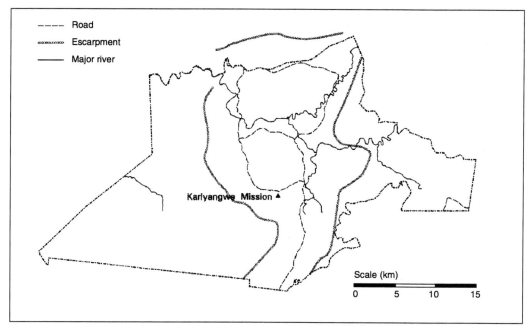

Figure 2. Kariyangwe study area

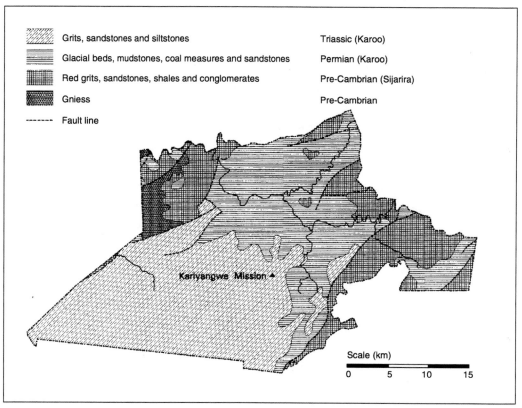

Figure 3. Geology of Kariyangwe

DATA SOURCES

Data have been acquired from various sources in Zimbabwe; tsetse distribution and control data have come from the Regional Tsetse and Trypanosomiasis

Control Programme (RTTCP) (Harare), topographical data from the Surveyor General (Harare), geological data from Geological Survey (Harare) and climatological data from published sources. Land cover and land use data have been extracted from historical Landsat Thematic Mapper and Multi-Spectral Scanner (MSS) data, dating from 1972 to 1993, from the EOSAT and Republic of South Africa remote sensing archives (Table 1).

Table 1. Data sources used in the study

Data Layer	Source	Scale	Factor
Land use 1972	MSS imagery	1:100 000	HDLU*, land cover
Land use 1976	MSS imagery	1:100 000	HDLU*, land cover
Land use 1984	TM imagery	1:50 000	HDLU*, land cover
Land use 1986	MSS imagery	1:100 000	HDLU*, land cover
Land use 1989	TM imagery	1:50 000	HDLU*, land cover
Land use 1993	TM imagery	1:50 000	HDLU*, land cover
Geology	Geological Survey	1:1M	Rock type
Roads	Surveyor General	1:250 000	3 km buffer
Ground spraying	RTTCP , Harare	1:250 000	spray years

* HDLU = Human dominated land use

Most of the data were of good quality, although a 1980 MSS image scanned from negatives proved unusable and no other satellite data for this period could be identified. This resulted in a considerable gap in coverages between 1976 and 1984.

METHODOLOGY

Fifteen distinct land cover classes were identified for the Lake Kariba study area from visual interpretation of 1992 cloud-free Landsat TM imagery and field surveys undertaken in the wet (February 1993) and dry (June 1993) seasons (Pender and Rosenberg, 1995). In order to simplify the analysis, TWINSPAN two-way variant analysis was used to reduce the number of land cover classes to six: human dominated land use (bare ground), grasses, woodland with single dominance *Colophospernum mopane*, woodland with *Combretum* spp., woodland with *Julbernadia globiflora*, and mixed woodland with no distinguishing species. The human dominated land use category (HDLU) included built-up areas, airstrips and cultivated and fallow fields. HDLU data, and a selection of other factors likely to be related to land use change, i.e., geology (a surrogate for soil type), natural vegetation cover, proximity to roads and tsetse control campaigns (number of sprays against tsetse), were combined in ARC/INFO GIS to give parcels of land with unique combinations of these factors for successive dates of satellite imagery (five study periods in Table 1). Tabular data relating to these land parcels were exported to a statistical package for further analysis.

For each study period, the total area in each possible combination of factors (natural vegetation cover, rock type, proximity to roads and number of sprayings) was calculated for each of the following categories:

(a) land not in HDLU at beginning of a period, but in use by the end;
(b) land not in HDLU at either the beginning or end of a period;
(c) land in HDLU at the beginning of a period but out of use at the end; and
(d) land in HDLU at both the beginning and end of a period.

For each combination of factors, the following were calculated using the quantities (a)-(d) above:

(1) percentage of the total amount of land which was unused by humans at the beginning of the period but was in HDLU by the end of the period; and
(2) percentage of the total amount of land that was HDLU at the beginning of the period but not in use at the end of the period.

In order to account for the variability of the percentages in (1) and (2) being inversely proportional to the size of the area on which they were based, each observation was weighted (each possible combination of vegetation type, rock type, proximity to roads and number of sprays constitutes an observation). For the analysis of the percentage of land brought into use (1), the weighting factor applied was the total area of land that was unused by humans at the beginning of the period for that observation. For the analysis of the percentage of land taken out of use (2), the weighting factor was the total area of land that was in use at the beginning of the period for that observation. Weighted regression was then applied to the data to identify which factors were most relevant for explaining the pattern of land use change in each study period.

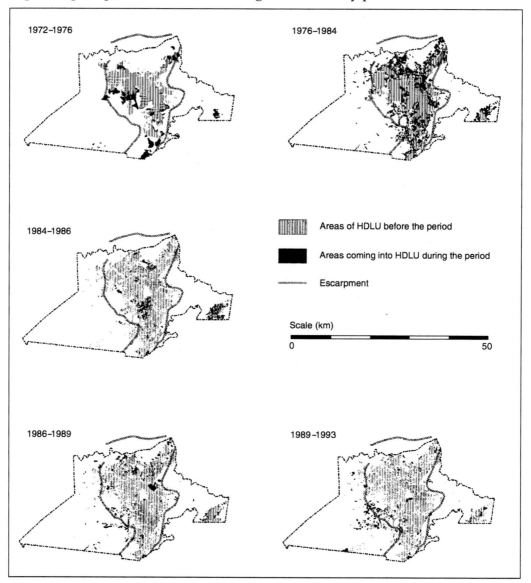

Figure 4. Increases in human dominated land use in Kariyangwe study area

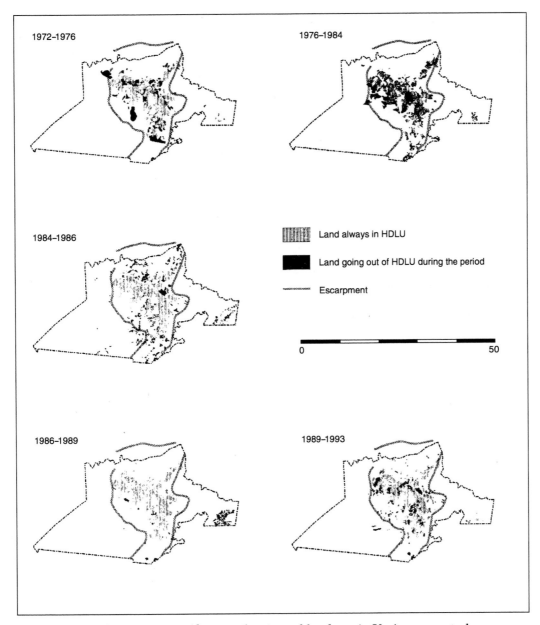

1972–1976

1976–1984

1984–1986

||||||| Land always in HDLU

■ Land going out of HDLU during the period

⁓⁓⁓ Escarpment

0   50

1986–1989

1989–1993

Figure 5. Land coming out of human dominated land use in Kariyangwe study area

RESULTS

Only 40 km² (2.4%) of the total area of Kariyangwe have been continuously under human dominated land use from1972 to1993, although the actual area being used at any one time varied between 123.8 (1972) and 155 km² (1989). Most of this land is concentrated in the basin (Figure 4).

Over the entire study period of 21 years, there has been a net increase in HDLU of only 15 km²; the most pronounced increases occurred between 1976 and 1984, and from 1986 to 1989 (Table 2). In the remaining periods, land in use was either relatively stable (1972–1976 and 1989–1993), or there was a net decrease in HDLU (1984–1986) (Table 2). The net figures, however, hide the spatial complexity of the land use changes during the entire study period. For example, between 1989 and 1993, there was a significant increase in HDLU for the first time above the escarpments surrounding the basin (Figure 4), while decreases in HDLU were almost exclusively confined to the basin (Figure 5).

Table 2. Areas of land being brought into, and taken out of, human dominated land use (HDLU) in Kariyangwe; the figure in brackets shows the mean area of change per year during that period

Period	Land bought into HDLU km^2 per period (per year)		Land taken out of HDLU km^2 per period (per year)	
1972–1976	31.6	(7.9)	31.8	(7.95)
1976–1984	84	(10.5)	59.1	(7.38)
1984–1986	16.6	(8.3)	25.3	(12.65)
1986–1989	22.8	(7.6)	7.5	(2.5)
1989–1993	16.6	(4.15)	23.1	(5.78)

For most of the study periods, increases in HDLU were related to proximity to roads and rock type (Table 3), although the relationship was relatively weak from 1984 to 1986, and from 1989 to 1993. Before 1986, most increases in HDLU occurred on the Permian (Karoo) glacial deposits, but from 1986 onwards, most HDLU increases were on Triassic (Karoo) grits in the southwest of the study area because land was no longer available on the valley glacial beds (Figure 4). The number of times tsetse control operations were carried out appears to be important only in the period 1972–1976 (Table 3).

Table 3. Relationship of human dominated land use (HDLU) to various factors and combinations of factors

Base Line 1972		1972–1976	1976–1984	1984–1986	1986–1989	1989–1993
road* rock rock x road	**Into Use**	**road** rock spray	**rock** vegetation road	**road** rock vegetation	**rock** vegetation vegetation x rock	**rock** road
	R^2†	82%	93%	40%	96%	50%
	Out of use	**spray** vegetation rock	**road** vegetation	**road** vegetation	**rock**	**vegetation** rock road
	R^2	91.4%	73%	67%	41%	83%

*Factors which show the most relevant relationship are shown in bold
†R^2 value refers to the % of the variability in the data which was explained by the model

To some extent, decreases in HDLU were related to proximity to roads or rock type in all the study periods between 1972 and 1993 (Table 3). Natural vegetation cover was only the most relevant of the variables tested from 1989 to 1993 when there was a marked decrease in HDLU in areas of mixed woodlands. HDLU increases and decreases affected higher proportions of *Colophospermum mopane* and mixed woodlands than any other vegetation cover class in all the study periods.

DISCUSSION AND CONCLUSIONS

In this study, remotely sensed data have been combined with other datasets in a GIS to quantify the changing distribution of human dominated land use in the Kariyangwe region of western Zimbabwe, and to analyse these changes in relation to a small sub-set of factors which might be relevant to changing land use patterns.

The results have shown that the pattern of land use change is both temporally and spatially complex. In general, the end of the War of Independence in 1980 and the improved security situation probably accounted for the significant expansion in HDLU between 1976 and 1984, while the drought from 1990 to 1992 may have resulted in a consolidation of land already under HDLU and a relatively small change in the area under HDLU. Proximity to roads appears to be an important factor influencing where land is brought into HDLU, and although many of the roads in the area have been improved to facilitate tsetse control operations in the past, tsetse control *per se* seems to be of minor significance in influencing land use change. Only in the 1972–1976 study period was the number of tsetse spray campaigns related to both increases and decreases in HDLU. Clearly, the small sub-set of variables studied here neither adequately defines the range of physical factors which influence where and when land use changes occur, nor describes the larger framework of socio-economic, developmental and planning factors which influence agricultural development.

The results of this study have provided a broad scale analysis of spatial and temporal patterns. The spatial analysis in particular illustrates a variability in land use change hidden by gross figures presented over time. Although the many factors which influence land use change were not studied, the selection of a small sub-set of relevant variables demonstrates the potential of this approach for interpreting land use changes.

ACKNOWLEDGEMENTS

This study was funded by the UK's Overseas Development Administration through the Livestock Production Programme. The authors would like to thank Ms S.Sian Floyd for the statistical analysis, and Dr L. J. Rosenberg for her guidance in the interpretation of the results and the production of this paper. The authors particularly appreciated the assistance of many organizations in Zimbabwe, including the Regional Tsetse and Trypanosomiasis Control Programme, the Surveyor General of Zimbabwe and the Geological Survey, for the use of their data in the survey, and Mr R. Drummond for identifying plants.

REFERENCES

Douthwaite, R.J. and Tingle, C.C.D. (eds) (1994) *DDT in the Tropics: the Impact on Wildlife in Zimbabwe of Ground Spraying for Tsetse Control.* Chatham, UK: Natural Resources Institute.

Hursey, B.S. and Allsopp, R. (1983) *Sequential Applications of Low Dosage Aerosols for Fixed Wing Aircraft as a Means of Eradicating Tsetse Flies* (Glossina spp.) *from Rugged Terrain in Zimbabwe.* Harare: Tsetse and Trypanosmiasis Branch, Department of Veterinary Services.

Lovemore, D.F. (1994) Overview of past and present tsetse distribution and control in Zimbabwe. pp. 5-25. In: *Proceedings of a Workshop to Co-ordinate Land-Use Change in the Zambezi Valley of Zimbabwe, Harare, 16-17 May 1994,* Harare: Regional Tsetse and Trypanosomiasis Control Programme and World Wide Fund for Nature. [Unpublished report.]

Pender, J. and Rosenberg, J. (1995) *Impact of Tsetse Control on Land Use in the Semi-Arid Zone of Zimbabwe; Phase 1: Classification of Land Use by Remote Sensing Imagery.* Natural Resources Institute Bulletin 66. Chatham, UK: Natural Resources Institute.

Prankherd, H.A. (1991) An economic comparison of land use systems appropriate for semi arid areas. *Project Appraisal,* 6(2): 93-99.

Using Landsat Thematic Mapper Data to Identify and Monitor Dambo Grassland and Water Resources

Rob Boast

Division of Geography, School of Sciences, Staffordshire University,
Leek Road, Stoke-on-Trent, ST3 2DF, UK.

ABSTRACT

Dambos are important resource features of the African savanna landscape. These shallow, seasonally saturated headwater depressions provide extensive pockets of high resource potential, in terms of water and fertile soils, within the sub-humid to sub-arid environments of Zimbabwe, Zambia and Malawi. Dambo grasslands can be identified, and their condition monitored, by using Landsat Thematic Mapper (TM) satellite imagery. The multi-spectral capabilities of the TM data allow the identification of the relatively moist, dark soils covered by actively photosynthesizing vegetation from surrounding cultivated interfluves. Coupled with this, the 30 m ground resolution allows not only identification of dambos but also, spatial variations in soil and vegetation conditions within them. Multi-temporal imagery can be used to monitor changes in water and vegetation conditions over the hydrological year, and the effect of resource management decisions, such as dambo cultivation or the cutting of woodland on interfluves, over the longer term.

INTRODUCTION

Dambos are areas of relative wetness within the seasonally dry savanna landscape of southern central Africa. These shallow, linear, headwater depressions, which are seasonally saturated and sustain grassland vegetation in contrast to the surrounding wooded interfluves, are important features of the landscape in terms of their hydrology, geomorphology and resource potential (Boast, 1990).

The aims of this paper are twofold; first, to outline the importance of dambos for supplying resources to local communities within semi-arid to sub-humid tropical landscapes of Africa, and secondly, to examine the potential role of satellite remote sensing in identifying, mapping, assessing the quality and monitoring the condition of dambo resources.

DAMBO RESOURCE POTENTIAL

Dambos represent a valuable natural resource to local human communities. Their relatively high water table and fertile clay soils provide high agricultural potential for grass meadows and crops. In Zimbabwe, winter dry season crops and summer crops in dry years are usually grown in small garden plots on the edges of dambos (Rattray et al., 1953; Whitlow, 1985; Windram et al., 1985). These 'gardens' are arranged down the cross-profile of the dambo slopes, across a range of soil conditions, so safeguarding the cultivator against complete agro-economic failure during times of environmental stress (Scoones, 1991). Dambos are extensively used for communal grazing of cattle and goats during the dry season, with the open channel at the lower end of the dambo being used as a water supply for livestock (Windram et al., 1985). They are also important as water supplies and for regulating river water flow (Mackel, 1985), although Bullock (1992a, 1992b) showed that in central Zimbabwe, they do not contribute significantly to dry season base-flows in rivers. Dambos are therefore clearly significant in providing water and agricultural resources for local communities within a landscape of lower resource potential. Their total resource potential is high as dambos and related landforms are found extensively over Africa (Figure 1), covering up to 30% of the landscape.

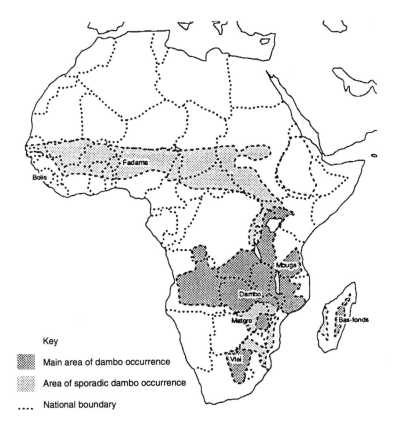

Figure 1. Distribution of dambos and related features within Africa (after Acres *et al.*, 1985)

It has to be recognized that there are increasing socio-economic pressures on dambos due to the growing demands for land for settlement, cultivation, grazing and mineral extraction. It is generally considered that removal of vegetation by firing, grazing or replacement with seasonally harvested crops will lead to increased soil erosion (Rattray *et al.*, 1953; Elwell and Davey, 1972; Whitlow, 1983, 1989). Trampling causes river bank collapse and compacts the soil, thus inducing run-off and gullying (Windram *et al.*, 1985).

Changes in land use on surrounding interfluves have indirectly impacted on dambos. The need for more land for cultivation on interfluves has led to the increasing use of dambos for year-round grazing. Faulkner and Lambert (1991) have suggested that the clearing of the interfluve woodland surrounding dambos in Zimbabwe's Communal Lands may have resulted in less evapotranspiration losses and thus to the maintenance of dambo water tables at higher levels for longer into the dry season.

As a consequence of fears about dambo degradation, Zimbabwe introduced legislation in 1927 and 1952 restricting their use for cultivation (Elwell and Davey, 1972; Whitlow, 1980; Windram *et al.*, 1985). Bell (1986) and Whitlow (1985, 1989) suggested that this legislation gave impetus to research on dambo management in Zimbabwe.

REMOTE SENSING OF DAMBO RESOURCES

The greatest potential use of remote sensing would appear to be in the management of resources in the tropical regions of the world. The repetitive coverage, consistent image quality, and image scale allow crop cover and hazard monitoring (Eden, 1986).

The Thematic Mapper (TM) on board the Landsat series of satellites meets several important criteria for identifying dambos. It records seven spectral wavebands which are used to target soil and vegetation conditions. Its nominal 30 m spatial resolution allows dambos, which are 1–10 km in length and up to 1 km in width, to be identified from surrounding interfluves, and enables the detection of internal variations in soil and vegetation. In addition, the 185 x 185 km image scenes allow regional variations in dambos to be studied, and the 16-day repeat period of the satellite provides the opportunity to monitor seasonal changes in the condition of dambos.

On-going research in Zimbabwe and Malawi has demonstrated that Landsat TM data imagery has the potential to be a valuable tool for the identification and mapping of dambo resources, the assessment of soil and vegetation resource quality, and monitoring changes in dambo resource conditions.

Identification of Dambo Resources

The accurate identification of dambos depends on them having a characteristic spectral response which is sufficiently different from the surrounding interfluves. On Landsat TM imagery of central Malawi taken in October (end of dry season) 1987, dambos within cultivated regions showed low red and high near infrared (NIR) radiance, indicative of a greater cover of healthy vegetation compared to the bare fields of the interfluves. They also had low near middle infrared (NMIR), middle infrared (MIR) and thermal infrared (TIR) responses, indicative of relatively moist, cool conditions.

Within the wooded Kasungu National Park, the grass-covered dambos showed relatively high radiance values for red, NMIR and TIR bands, and low NIR radiance. This was indicative of a low cover of healthy vegetation compared to the interfluve woodland.

Assessment of Dambo Soil and Vegetation

Boast and Bullock (1995) and Boast (1995) have established that there are consistent relationships between dambo physical properties and surface radiance for a sample of dambos in central Zimbabwe. The main findings are listed below.

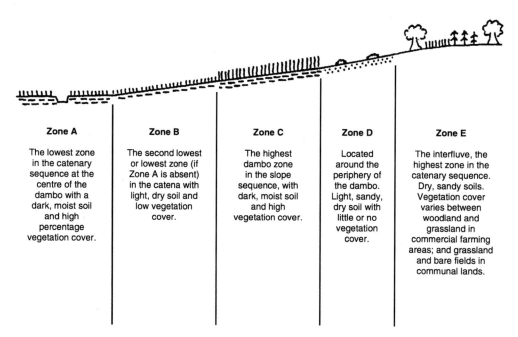

Zone A	Zone B	Zone C	Zone D	Zone E
The lowest zone in the catenary sequence at the centre of the dambo with a dark, moist soil and high percentage vegetation cover.	The second lowest or lowest zone (if Zone A is absent) in the catena with light, dry soil and low vegetation cover.	The highest dambo zone in the slope sequence, with dark, moist soil and high vegetation cover.	Located around the periphery of the dambo. Light, sandy, dry soil with little or no vegetation cover.	The interfluve, the highest zone in the catenary sequence. Dry, sandy soils. Vegetation cover varies between woodland and grassland in commercial farming areas; and grassland and bare fields in communal lands.

Figure 2. Soil and vegetation zones identified along the dambo-interfluve catena

1.   The dambos displayed distinct soil and vegetation zones (Figure 2) identified by Faulkner and Lambert (1991) and termed hydro-pedological zones.

2.   In the Communal Lands, dambos which were heavily grazed had much lower vegetation biomass and cover values than lightly grazed dambos in commercial farming areas.

3.   Consistent and significant relationships were found between the soil and vegetation variables and the reflectance data recorded by a hand-held radiometer.

4.   Consistent relationships were also obtained for the soil and vegetation data with the Landsat TM radiance values.

Monitoring Dambo Conditions

By definition, dambos are dominated by seasonal changes in their soil and vegetation condition. To examine these changes, two Landsat TM images of central Malawi were used, one from October 1987 (end of dry season) and one from May 1988 (start of the following dry season). The two images were geometrically registered and radiance values corrected for differences in sun angle.

The following 'hypotheses' were tested.

1. Are dambos easier to identify at the beginning of the dry season than at the end?

Drayton (1986) suggested that the contrast between the relatively wetter dambos and the surrounding interfluves would increase as the dry season progressed. This was tested by sampling 30 dambos from the whole quarter scene of central Malawi, recording the radiance in the TM bands for the dambos and the immediately adjacent interfluves for the October 1987 and May 1988 images. It was found that the contrast in radiance for TM 1-7 between dambo and interfluve was indeed greater at the end than at the start of the dry season. This seems to confirm the findings of Drayton (1986).

2. Are the hydro-pedological zones identified at the end of the dry season maintained as distinct zones at the start of the following dry season?

Eighty dambos were sampled from the image area and the radiance values from both images were recorded for dry centres, wet margins and surrounding interfluves. The radiance values were combined to provide indices of healthy vegetation (NIR–Red / NIR + Red, see Tucker, 1979) and moisture stress (NMIR/NIR, see Lundén and Fagerlund, 1985; Frazier, 1989; Hunt and Rock, 1989).

First, the data showed that for each of the landscape components, dambo and interfluve, there was a significant increase in the vegetation index and decrease in the moisture stress index from October 1987 to May 1988 (Figure 3). This would indicate that the general environment has a greater cover of healthy vegetation, and is wetter, at the start of a dry season than at the end.

Secondly, the data showed that for the dambos in the cultivated region, the 'dry' centres in the October 1987 image had disappeared in the May 1988 image. Indeed, in May 1988, the former 'dry' centre areas had higher vegetation index values and lower moisture stress index values than the adjacent former 'wet' margins. This would seem to suggest that at the start of a dry season, the wettest areas with the greatest cover of healthy vegetation were the dambo centres which then dried out by the end of a dry season. This could mean that the model proposed by Faulkner and Lambert (1991) relating to seasonal hydrological fluctuation based on dambos in central Zimbabwe might also be applicable to central Malawi.

3. Does removal of interfluve woodland lead to differences in the radiance of dambos?

This should ideally be investigated by examining image data of a dambo catchment before and after tree clearing. However, as much of the tree clearing in central southern Africa pre-dates satellite imagery, this was not possible. Instead, two areas of different interfluve land use were identified and compared within the Malawi image: cultivated interfluves mainly cleared of trees; and the Kasungu National Park which retains its wooded cover. It is appreciated that factors other than interfluve management, e.g. soil type and topography, may vary and therefore account for differences in dambo conditions between the two sample regions.

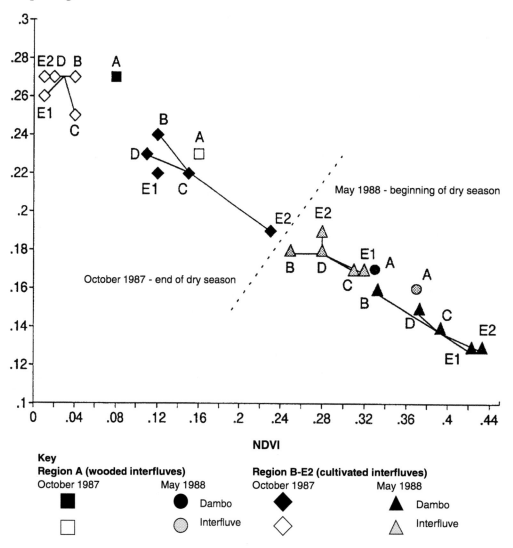

Figure 3. The seasonal changes in mean NDVI and Moisture Stress (Dry) Index values for dambo and interfluve components from wooded and cultivated sample regions

Using the previous data, Figure 3 indicates that dambos within the cultivated region would appear to be wetter (lower moisture stress index values) and have a greater cover of healthy vegetation (higher vegetation index values) than dambos in the wooded game reserve, both at the end and the start of the dry season. Such a situation would be consistent with the removal of trees, resulting in a reduction in evapotranspiration losses from the catchment and thus enabling maintenance of high water tables for the dambos in the cultivated regions. These observations are consistent with those envisaged by Faulkner and Lambert (1991) for dambos in central Zimbabwe.

CONCLUSION

Dambos are relatively rich resource features providing water, crops and grazing within a generally much drier and less fertile landscape. These pockets of resource are quite extensive in area and are very important to local communities. Due to increasing pressure, however, there is a growing risk of their degradation, and an increasing need for appropriate management based on sound resource assessment. Remote sensing has the potential to be a valuable tool in this regard.

The results presented here are encouraging in that Landsat TM images can be used to identify and map the location of dambos as well as the spatial variations in soil and vegetation within them. There appear to be consistent relationships between the soil and vegetation conditions and the radiance values recorded both by a hand-held radiometer and the Landsat TM sensor. Seasonal changes in the condition of dambos can be assessed using multi-temporal imagery.

The effects of human impacts on the dambo landscape can also be assessed. The effect on dambo radiance of variations in vegetation cover resulting from cattle grazing can be readily identified on imagery. Similarly, the impact on the dambo water table resulting from the removal of trees from surrounding interfluves results in changes in dambo radiance.

The main benefit of remote sensing for dambo studies is that it enables, with a greater degree of confidence, the spatial extrapolation of ideas and models based on samples of relatively few dambos previously surveyed on the ground.

ACKNOWLEDGEMENTS

Much of the research for this paper was carried out as part of a D.Phil. thesis sponsored by the NERC (research award GT4/87/GS/90) and conducted jointly at the School of Geography, University of Oxford and the Institute of Hydrology, Wallingford.

REFERENCES

Acres, B.D., Blair-Rain, A., King, B., Lawton, R.M.,. Mitchell, A.J.B and Rackham, L.J. (1985) African dambos: their distribution, characteristics and use. *Zeitschrift für Geomorphologie*, **52**: 63-86.

Bell, M. (1986) Irrigation: drive to develop dambos (wetlands in Zimbabwe). *World Water*, **9** (2): 13.

Boast, R. (1990) Dambos: a review. *Progress in Physical Geography*, **14**(2): 153-177.

Boast, R. (1995) *The identification of hydro-pedological zones within dambos of central Zimbabwe using Landsat Thematic Mapper data.* [Unpublished.]

Boast, R. and Bullock, A. (1995) *The potential of remote sensing for the spatial extrapolation of dambo vegetation, soil and hydrological properties.* [Unpublished.]

Bullock, A. (1992a) Dambo hydrology in southern Africa - review and reassessment. *Journal of Hydrology*, **134**(1-4): 373-396.

Bullock, A. (1992b) The role of dambos in determining river flow regimes in Zimbabwe. *Journal of Hydrology*, **134**(1-4): 349-372.

Drayton, R.S. (1986) Dambo hydrology - an application of satellites remote sensing to water resource studies in the Third World. In: *Proceedings of the International Symposium on Mapping from Modern Imagery, The Remote Sensing Society, 8-12 September 1986, Edinburgh.*

Eden, M. J. (1986) The management of renewable resources in the Tropics: the use of remote sensing. pp. 3-16. In: Eden, M.J. and Parry, J.T. (eds) *Remote Sensing and Tropical Land Management.* London: Wiley.

Elwell, H.A. and Davey, C.J.N. (1972) Vlei cropping and soil and water resources. *Rhodesian Agriculture Journal Technical Bulletin*, **15**: 155-168.

Faulkner, R.D. and Lambert, R.A. (1991) The effect of irrigation on dambo hydrology. *Journal of Hydrology*, **123**: 147-161.

Frazier, B.E. (1989) Use of Landsat Thematic Mapper band ratios for soil investigations. *Advances in Space Research*, **9**(1): 155-158.

Hunt, E.R. Jr and Rock, B.N. (1989) Detection of changes in leaf water content using near-and middle-infrared reflectances. *Remote Sensing of the Environment*, **30**(1): 43-54.

Lundén, B. and Fagerlund, E. (1985) A comparison between Landsat-TM data and ground measured radiance and soil data. *Proceedings of the 3rd International Colloquium on Spectral Signatures of Objects in Remote Sensing, Les Arcs, France 16-20 December 1985.*

Mackel, R. (1985) Dambos and related landform in Africa. *Zeitschrift für Geomorphologie*, **52**: 1-23.

Rattray, J.M., Cormack, R.M.M. and Staples, R.R. (1953) The vlei areas of Southern Rhodesia and their uses. *Rhodesia Agriculture Journal*, **50**: 465-483.

Scoones, I. (1991) *Wetlands in Drylands: the Agroecology of Savanna Systems in Africa - Part 1.* London: International Institute for Environment and Development.

Tucker, C.J. (1979) Red and photographic infrared linear combinations for monitoring vegetation. *Remote Sensing of the Environment*, **8**: 127-150.

Whitlow, J.R. (1980) The morphology of two different vleis on the highveld of Zimbabwe Rhodesia. *Zimbabwe-Rhodesia Agriculture Journal*, **77**: 71-80.

Whitlow, J.R. (1983) Vlei cultivation in Zimbabwe reflections on the past. *Zimbabwe Agriculture Journal*, **80**(3): 125-135.

Whitlow, J.R. (1985) Dambos in Zimbabwe. A review. *Zeitschrift für Geomorphologie*, **52**: 115-146.

Whitlow, J.R. (1989) *Gullying Within Dambos, With Particular Reference To The Communal Farming Areas Of Zimbabwe.* Ph.D thesis [unpublished]. UK: University of London.

Windram, A. F., Faulkner, R., Bell, M., Roberts, N., Hotchkiss, P. and Lamber, R. (1985) The use of dambos in small scale rural development. pp. 114-117. In: *Proceedings of the 11th WEDC Conference: Water and Sanitation in Africa, Dar es Salaam, Tanzania, 15-19 April 1985.*

PANEL DISCUSSION

Finding a Way Forward

Gesche Schmid-McGibbon[1] and Judith Pender[2]
[1]University of Greenwich, Chatham Maritime, Chatham, Kent UK.
[2]Natural Resources Institute, Central Avenue, Chatham Maritime, Chatham, Kent, ME4 4TB, UK.

Chaired by: Ian Downey, Robert Ridgway and Jim Williams (NRI)

INTRODUCTION

A panel discussion was organized to identify key areas of good practice, constraints or opportunities, to enable the progression of remote sensing (RS) and geographical information systems (GIS) for natural resource management. The aim was to identify those factors which are enabling RS and GIS techniques to become a mature, integrated, reliable, transferable and acceptable discipline. The discussion was structured around three main items:

- problem solving
- implementation issues
- investment in machines versus people or training.

The chairman, Ian Downey, identified the following questions for discussion under these headings.

1. Problem solving
    - Is there a demand for information?
    - Does the quality of the information delivered lead to better informed decisions?
    - Are time series data important for natural resource monitoring?
    - Are we getting the balance right between the technology and the information delivered to the users?
    - Does a common analysis technique exist between developing and developed countries?

2. Implementation issues
    - What are the constraints to effective implementation of RS and GIS for natural resource management?
    - How can the RS and GIS community better assist potential users to adopt these techniques?

3. Investment machines versus people
    - Is investment in equipment the most effective means of furthering the uptake of RS and GIS for natural resource management?
    - Is it more effective to develop training materials and activities to assist potential users in identifying and implementing their appropriate RS/GIS solutions?

Many of these issues were addressed in presentations by keynote speakers and conference delegates, especially the practical issues of problem solving. Much of the panel discussion was concerned with exploring issues of implementation and training. A synthesis of the main points of the discussion is presented in this summary.

IMPLEMENTATION

Cost of data, especially imagery, was identified as a major constraint to the implementation of RS and GIS projects. For example, the cost of high resolution imagery varies according to how, and by whom, the data are being bought. One of the panel members likened purchasing RS imagery to buying a ticket on a jumbo jet, where passengers on adjacent seats will have paid different prices. However, large volume customers can develop purchasing strategies. The purchasing policy for the EC-funded MARS project, for example, kept prices down by ordering data centrally for the Europe-wide project, even though elements of the project were carried out in different countries. This might be a useful strategy for aid agencies and donors to follow. It was also pointed out that information on low-cost data sources and software has been published, in one of the back issues of the Geology Remote Sensing Group newsletter for example.

Although RS and GIS are often seen as expensive tools for solving problems, several examples of savings using the technology were provided by the panel. In 1995, for example, the EC spent 15 million Ecu on RS and GIS to control fraud in Europe but collected 100 million Ecu in fines. In the United States, the agricultural service of the USDA set the value for one TM scene as the US$ 20 million that were saved by identifying fraudulent claims during a Mississippi flood. Similarly, 150 million Ecu were saved on every decision based on information from the MARS project (the project cost 35 million Ecu over 5 years). It has proved more difficult to demonstrate cost-benefit in the developing world as comparable base level figures are not available.

In addition to the previous point, one panel member stated that guidelines for selecting an appropriate system are lacking. Before purchasing a system, questions have to be answered on the capabilities and functions needed to fulfil set objectives.

Accuracy assessment was one of the main topics of discussion. Members of the panel felt that the implementation of RS and GIS suffers from the lack of such assessments. In the developed world, the user often demands to know the precision of data (e.g. MARS project) whereas in developing countries, the problem is often not addressed. However, the measurement of accuracies may be neglected because it will add to the cost of a project. There was some debate on whether field sampling patterns and accuracy algorithms developed in Europe were appropriate when applied to problems in the developing world where areas are larger and boundaries indistinct. Provided allowances are made for local conditions, methods are transferable because a standard image product and uniform philosophy of statistical calibration exist. It was pointed out that a measured accuracy of about 60% is usually attained in studies using remotely sensed data from all sources, including aerial photography. Aid agencies should be made aware of the effect on results of calibration work. It was felt that calibration should be more widely accepted as a valid project cost.

Desktop remote sensing was unthinkable a few years ago, but one panel member envisaged its widespread use in the near future. This will have a liberating effect on data usage, but in order to facilitate access to data, it will be necessary to set up a re-selling data network with access to an exhaustive meta database.

Accessibility to data is already changing dramatically due to improved networking and cataloguing capabilities.

INVESTMENT IN MACHINES VERSUS PEOPLE

In the developing world, aid agencies support sustainable development and foster interest in environmental issues. RS and GIS technologies are powerful analysis tools for solving problems. The aim has to be one of persuading clients that RS/GIS can solve problems in a cost-effective way. Although the total cost of GIS and RS in comparison to a country's total development budget is minimal (1–2 %), users relate the cost of equipment and data to their personal salaries. It is therefore necessary to educate the decision makers and users to the benefit of investing in the technology. Some aid agencies finance short-course training at director level. Indonesia provides a good example for demonstrating how awareness of GIS and RS can be developed through training. It has taken 10 years, and a lot of money, to train people at B.Sc., M.Sc. and Ph.D. level to obtain a return on the initial investment.

The panel pointed out that the ways in which RS and GIS data are presented as information to decision makers has to change. Decisions have to be made on the best available data and will not be used if the decision maker does not understand the relevance of the information provided. The data have to be in an accessible and attractive form which is readily understood. For example, lay people may understand a map showing sea surface temperature but not necessarily one showing vegetation indices; we therefore have to provide information in recognizable components. Public awareness of GIS and RS has to be increased if these tools are to be adopted more widely for natural resource management.

Training on short courses of one week's duration is not enough to train people in the implementation methods for generating usable information. This training takes much longer, at least a year. More education and training is needed on how to use the information rather than on how to generate more and more data. In general, education is not broad enough to reach the general public or decision makers. Furthermore, refresher training is needed for people educated many years ago, to enable them to use more complex technology.

In the future, the focus has to change from the outside provision of training to the support of internal facilitators. Significant results can be obtained, with a small investment, from the establishment of self-help and support groups for organizing meetings, training courses and newsletters. Students from developing countries are focused, motivated, and show a willingness to teach themselves or learn from one another. This motivation must be encouraged.

ODA has supported sustainable development since 1968. Many reports created by the land resource department from 1968 to 1988 have not been followed up. ODA considers the most successful project proposals to be the ones which identify a problem with solutions rather than those which are technology led.

Development agencies realize that there is need for small-scale participatory approaches, and that information has to be disseminated to small rural communities. GIS and RS are well suited to such an approach because they are structured and rigid technologies which have an active part to play in providing information to the rural community.

RS and GIS can be used as active tools in the community for data management and data resources. Hard copy Landsat imagery has been used to define village boundaries and grazing boundaries. People in rural communities could relate this to their own areas better than when using traditional maps. Features could be identified more readily when images were placed on the ground rather than presented vertically. Conversely, it was argued that rural communities in developing countries often have a mature understanding of their environment and do not need to use satellite imagery to produce maps. However, RS imagery is an independent source of information and people can relate to a picture much more easily than to an abstract map.

RS in the developing world is practical at village level. At the other end of the scale, large donor agencies of mapping projects have been successfully acting at the central government level. At the middle administrative level, however, at which donor money is often targeted, the record of implementation is not as good. There is a need to promote RS and GIS where the techniques work, and to establish the reasons for the lack of success elsewhere. The key is to involve local people so that outputs are used rather than left on a shelf.

One of the chairs, Jim Williams, summed up at the end of the panel discussion and made the following comments.

1. The private sector has to address real problems and real needs in order to survive. In the future, the private sector may have a larger role to play in small- or medium-sized enterprises in developing countries.
2. There is a very clear need for an integrated approach, and the opportunity exists for RS and GIS to be involved in this approach. The integrated approach remains difficult to sell to donor agencies because of its complexity.

Satellite Spectral Input to a Moorland Management Model

G. G. Wright, J. G. Morrice and J. S. Allison

Macaulay Land Use Research Institute, Craigiebuckler, Aberdeen, AB9 2QJ.

Satellite remote sensing is now considered a feasible way of monitoring moorland resources. A further advance would be to use the satellite-derived vegetation assessments as a source of data for moorland management needs.

The first aim of this study is to use Landsat TM Spectral information (Photo), in the form of an unsupervised spectral classification and normalized vegetation index data (Table 1) to increase the spatial knowledge of spectrally and ecologically meaningful semi-natural vegetation types, appropriate to grazing management. Accuracy and reliability were measured against ground truth information, visual image assessments and the Land Cover of Scotland 1988 (LCS88) data set (Table 2).

Table 1. Landsat spectral mean, range and standard deviations for the unsupervised vegetation spectral classes

Table 2. Pixel by pixel comparison of satellite spectral classes and LCS88 cover features or groups

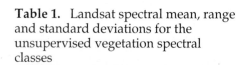

Vegetation cover spectrally defined	Stats.	Landsat TM waveband					Vegetation index
		TM1	TM2	TM3	TM4	TM5	NDVI*
1. Water bodies	Mean	3.3	2.7	3.8	9.8	14.9	37.4**
	St. dev.	2.0	1.2	2.2	7.1	8.5	17.6**
2. Undiff. woodlands	Mean	4.9	4.7	5.1	41.3	30.3	76.0
	St. dev.	1.18	1.3	1.6	6.2	5.9	5.4
3. Calluna moorland	Mean	5.8	5.1	8.0	37.8	49.6	64.7
	St. dev.	2.1	1.3	1.9	4.5	4.3	7.8
4. Eriophorum, Tricophorum Blanket bog	Mean	8.8	7.3	12.0	40.6	61.2	54.2
	St. dev.	2.2	1.5	2.3	4.8	3.7	6.7
5. Sphagnum (Blanket bog)	Mean	12.2	10.1	16.5	46.2	72.8	47.7
	St. dev.	2.6	1.7	2.9	5.1	4.8	7.4
6. Imp. pasture (mod. quality)	Mean	11.6	11.1	12.9	72.9	74.1	68.9
	St. dev.	2.6	1.9	3.6	7.5	8.8	8.3
7. Imp. pasture (good quality)	Mean	8.7	9.3	7.2	99.7	66.7	84.1
	St. dev.	2.1	1.4	2.1	8.7	7.8	3.7
8. Nat. grassland and imp. pasture (v. poor quality)	Mean	15.9	13.3	21.0	56.5	88.6	47.6
	St. dev.	2.9	2.2	3.6	6.7	7.5	6.8
9. Imp. pasture (poor quality)	Mean	16.6	15.3	19.8	82.9	97.6	60.2
	St. dev.	3.7	2.7	5.1	7.9	8.5	8.2

Satellite spectral and visually defined vegetation classes	LCS88 cover groups as percentage area of spectral class					
	All woodland	Dry h. moor	Wet h. moor	Blanket bog	Impoved pasture	Natural grassland
1. Water bodies*	—	4.00	—	20.00	20.00	—
2. Undiff. woodlands	90.24	5.69	—	0.49	2.04	1.24
3. Calluna moorland	5.61	55.24	2.89	33.16	1.00	2.07
4. Eriophorum, Tricophorum Blanket bog	1.66	31.78	4.95	57.71	1.32	2.48
5. Sphagnum (Blanket bog)	1.74	31.68	1.56	55.88	4.26	4.81
6. Imp. pasture (mod. quality)	14.04	4.81	1.43	11.41	52.70	15.62
7. Imp. pasture (good quality)	6.87	2.22	—	9.09	81.37	0.44
8. Nat. grassland and imp. pasture (v. poor quality)	2.18	30.23	1.09	26.71	18.47	21.31
9. Imp. pasture (poor quality)	2.13	21.81	—	10.74	40.64	24.67

*   NDVI – Normalized Difference Vegetation Index
**   Estimate for water bodies based on data outwith the 'Bogeney Estate' test due to the insufficient area of the cover features within

Undiff – Includes all coniferous, deciduous and scrub woodland
Imp. – Improved - selectively managed or fertilized, often re-seeded
Nat. – Natural - includes Smooth, Nardus, Malinia, Rush and undiffentiated natural grassland communities

*   Reliable estimate for water bodies not possible due to insufficient area of cover feature within the test area of 'Bogeney Estate'

H.Moor – Heather moorland
Undiff – Includes all coniferous, deciduous and scrub woodland
Imp. – Improved - selectively managed or fertilized, often re-seeded
Nat. – Natural - includes Smooth, Nardus, Malinia, Rush and undiffentiated natural grassland communities

A second aim of the study was to test the usefulness of the spectral classification as an input to the MLURI Heather Moorland Management Model (HMMM) (Figure 1). This was tested by assessing the sheep carrying capacity of an imaginary estate (Figure 2), using both the satellite and the LCS88 land cover information (Tables 3 and 4).

Figure 1. Modified HMMM structure

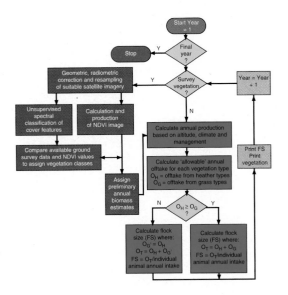

Figure 2. Diagrammatic representation of vegetation cover derived from satellite data smoothed with a 9 x 9 majority filter

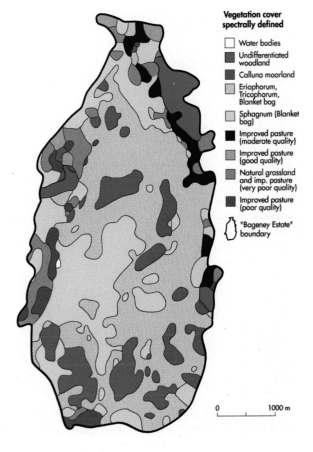

Vegetation cover spectrally defined

- Water bodies
- Undifferentiated woodland
- Calluna moorland
- Eriophorum, Tricophorum, Blanket bog
- Sphagnum (Blanket bog)
- Improved pasture (moderate quality)
- Improved pasture (good quality)
- Natural grassland and imp. pasture (very poor quality)
- Improved pasture (poor quality)
- "Bogeney Estate" boundary

0   1000 m

Table 3. Biomass and stocking density estimated for LCS88 land cover features

LCS88 cover group	Area (Ha)	Calculated biomass (kg/DM/ha/y)*	Utilisation (%)	Total usable biomass (kg/DM/y)
Water	1.16	—	—	—
Woodlands	104.40	—	—	—
Dry heather moor	547.44	1600	30	262,770
Wet heather moor	48.00	2000	20	19,200
Blanket bog	752.20	1400	10	105,310
Improved pasture*	111.84	3370	75	282,675
Natural grassland	86.80	2190	30	57,030

*(LCS88 Improved pasture has no quality assessment attached to it, so we have assumed a moderate production)

Total biomass production for the estate
= 726 985 kg/DM/y
Grassland biomass production
= 339 705 kg/DM/y
Non-grassland biomass production
= 387 280 kg/DM/y
40% non-grassland biomass production
= 154 910 kg/DM/y

Sheep stocking
Grassland vegetation limiting
with 50% feed from non-grassland
= 1510 or 0.91 ewe/ha
with 40% utilization of non-grassland vegetation
= 1510 or 0.91 ewe/ha
or 100% feed from grassland
= 755 or 0.46 ewe/ha

Table 4. Biomass and stocking density estimates for satellite spectral vegetation cover classes

Satellite cover group	Area (Ha)	Calculated biomass (kg/DM/ha/y)*	Utilisation (%)	Total usable biomass (kg/DM/y)
Water	1.00	—	—	—
Woodlands	64.76	—	—	—
Dry heather moor	276.48	1600	30	132,710
Wet heather moor	620.56	2000	20	248,225
Blanket bog	463.16	1400	10	64,840
Improved (poor) pasture (mod) (good)	37.60 / 53.28 / 18.04	2780 / 3370 / 5520	65 / 75 / 85	67,945 / 134,665 / 84,645
Natural grassland	116.96	2190	30	76,845

Total biomass production for the estate
= 809 875 kg/DM/y
Grassland biomass production
= 364 100 kg/DM/y
Non-grassland biomass production
= 445 775 kg/DM/y
40% non-grassland biomass production
= 178 310 kg/DM/y

Sheep stocking
Grassland vegetation limiting
with 50% feed from non-grassland
= 1618 or 0.98 ewe/ha
with 40% utilization of non-grassland vegetation
= 1206 or 0.73 ewe/ha
or 100% feed from grassland
= 809 or 0.49 ewe/ha

POSTERS

The Determination of the Most Appropriate Wavelengths for Research into Remote Sensing of Water Quality Parameters in Case II Waters

Alex Moon

Middlesex University, Department of Geography and Environmental Management GIS Laboratory, Middlesex University, Queensway, Enfield, Middlesex EN3 4SF, UK.

ABSTRACT

Past research into coastal and marine applications of remote sensing has been restricted to the use of a handful of wavebands which existing sensors have provided. This situation is changing, and will continue to change, with the gradual increase in available satellites and sensors specifically designed for marine applications, e.g. MERIS and SeaWIFS, and with the increasing interest in the use of airborne spectroradiometers. The technology of using relatively low-cost airborne spectroradiometers could provide a method for effectively monitoring pollution along local coastal areas, especially if these areas are of particular scientific, economic or environmental interest. The poster presentation shows some of the first results from PhD field work carried out between August and September 1995 at Southend-on-Sea. The field data were collected using a field spectroradiometer (supplied by the NERC) and taking simultaneous water quality samples. The initial water quality parameters of interest were those identified by the EU for monitoring bathing water, but some additional parameters which influence the spectral characteristics of coastal waters, such as chlorophyll-a, have been included.

INTRODUCTION

Public awareness of environmental issues over the last decade has increased. This has led to an increase in the importance of ensuring that water quality around our coasts is maintained at an acceptable level. To maintain water quality, methods of monitoring have to be applied. The European Union (EU) has directives on both bathing water and shellfish water quality, and the National Rivers Authority (NRA) is responsible for monitoring these levels. It is common for local authorities (during the summer season) to carry out their own monitoring programmes in an effort to prove that their water is clean. Some larger industries may also carry out their own environmental monitoring around local sites in order to avoid bad publicity and possible prosecution.

This project aims to provide data on the most appropriate wavelengths and wavebands for research into monitoring or measuring EU water quality parameters by remote sensing in our highly turbid coastal waters (Case II waters). This could form one of the first stages towards a method of yielding coastal water quality data from remote sensing using high spectral resolution instruments.

THE RESEARCH SETTING

Most studies into water quality parameters have been concerned with a single criterion such as chlorophyll or sediment load. For a monitoring system to be useful and cost effective, it must be able to study many parameters required by the various organizations involved in water quality. The EU directives (Johnson *et al.*, 1989; Department of Environment, 1989) are the best starting point for the development of a monitoring system since they provide a limited number of parameters, with recommended or required levels and instructions on how and when these should be monitored. These parameters give a clear indication of what would be required for a remote sensing monitoring system.

It would obviously be ideal if the water quality parameters could be identified directly from remotely sensed data and this would have to be the primary aim of a monitoring method. However, in most cases, this may not be possible because the effect on spectral reflectance of a water quality parameter may be small or indistinguishable from the effects of other parameters. In many cases, it is likely that secondary characteristics of a pollutant could be identified using remote sensing and this would then indicate the presence of the pollutant (see Figure 1). Indeed "many important water characteristics such as dissolved oxygen, phosphorus, and salt concentration cannot be observed directly through changes in water reflectance......such parameters sometimes correlate with observed reflectance. In short, there are many complex interrelationships between the spectral reflectance of water and particular characteristics" (Lillesand *et al.*,1987).

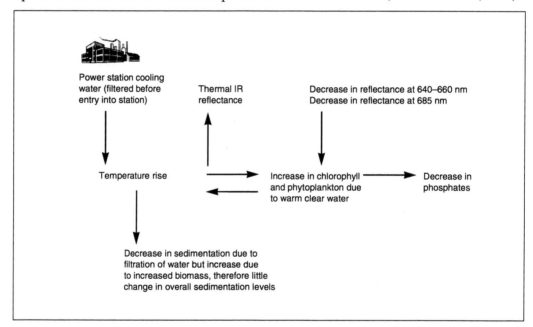

Figure 1. Fictional example of spectral model of a water quality parameter (temperature)

THE RESEARCH CHALLENGE

Past research into remote sensing has been restricted to the use of a handful of wavebands provided by existing sensors. This has been an underlying reason for the slow progress of research into marine applications. Typically, satellite programmes such as SPOT, Landsat and ERS were designed for terrestrial applications. This situation is changing, and will continue to change, with the gradual increase in available satellites and sensors such as MERIS and SeaWIFS. There is also an increasing interest in the use of airborne spectroradiometers. Relatively low-cost airborne spectroradiometer technology could provide an effective method of monitoring local coastal areas, especially those of particular scientific, economic or environmental interest.

It is against this background of the increasing potential and use of airborne spectroradiometers, photography and video, and the impending SeaWIFS and MERIS satellites, that a method of monitoring water quality in Case II waters can be set. Spectroradiometers such as CASI (Canadian Airborne Spectrographic Instrument) allow the collection of spectral data at almost any wavelength. This means that spectral reflectance at very precise wavelengths can be recorded (CASI has a maximum 1.8 nm resolution). The increased choice of wavebands which can be selected for data collection has meant that there is a need to ascertain which wavelengths would be genuinely useful. This would allow spectral reflectance recordings to be made in only a few selected spectral channels.

The benefits of research into the derivation of optimal wavelengths and wavebands for monitoring EU water quality parameters in Case II waters can be summarized into two categories.

- **Optimal wavelengths** can be used in research, and in systems using airborne or laboratory spectroradiometers, to allow increased spatial resolution and/or eliminate data redundancy in both data collection and analysis. The use of spectroradiometers allows the collection of spectral data through a wide range of individual wavelengths and therefore data redundancy is a significant problem. Accuracy can be increased with increased spatial resolution. Alternatively, spatial resolution can be maintained at the same level and the time for both data collection and analysis reduced significantly.

- **Optimal wavebands** derived from the optimal wavelengths can be used by researchers to select data from satellites/sensors which provide the closest fit to the wavebands identified for Case II water quality.

SELECTION OF WATER QUALITY PARAMETERS

The EU water quality parameters for bathing and shellfish waters were initially taken as the parameters of interest. Parameters were removed or added to this list on the basis of previous studies which looked at individual parameters in other environments. Others, e.g. heavy metals, were removed from consideration because the levels involved were very low and would therefore have negligible effects on the composition of the water and its spectral characteristics. The only way such parameters can be monitored is by relating them to other side effect parameters, e.g. their effect on the ecosystem. Other parameters, such as chlorophyll-a and ammonia nitrogen, were included because of their significance to the coastal ecosystem and the fact that they are monitored by the NRA in rivers and freshwater areas. Ultimately, a preliminary list of 15 water quality parameters was selected for study in the initial field work (see Table 1). This list had to be kept to a practical length because of the time restraints on completing the laboratory work while the samples were still fresh. The tidal state and weather conditions were also recorded.

DATA COLLECTION

The reflectance of the water was measured using a field spectroradiometer (GER SIRIS) from two stationed points at the end of the Southend-on-Sea pier which is approximately 2 km off-shore. The pier had three major advantages: it offered a stable platform over coastal water next to a beach designated as EU bathing water and could provide water in excess of 4 m at any tidal state; there was no delay in getting water samples to the laboratory for analysis; and the pier could be used to provide a barrier against direct sunlight so that problems with surface glare could be ignored. The spectroradiometer was held approximately 3 m

Table 1

Parameter	Effects and importance	Examples of relations
Dissolved oxygen	It is affected by temperature, organic matter, photosynthetic activity, bacterial oxygen activity. Oxygen required for oxidation of sewage, ammonia to nitrogen, etc. Some sewage discharges are supersaturated with oxygen through treatment.	photosynthesis bacterial temp (high=high) nitrate levels oxidation
BOD	Decomposition by aerobic bacteria of organic (including sewage) and nitrogenous material requires oxygen, this means a high BOD. A high BOD is indicative of pollution, particularly sewage.	organic material sewage=high nitrogenous material
Salinity	Tidal state and industrial and domestic drainage.	
Alkalinity	High alkalinity complexes heavy metals, reducing their toxicity.	heavy metals ammonia nitrogen
Ammonia nitrogen	Indicator of domestic and industrial waste.	oxygen organic matter
Temperature	Rise in temperature will increase biodegradation of organic material. Therefore will increase BOD.	oxygen chlorophyll
Suspended solids	Detrimental to aesthetic enjoyment. Chemically they can reduce the DO content of water if they are predominantly organic. If inorganic, they can reduce the BOD by effectively smothering the biomass.	colour BOD chlorophyll turbidity
Phenols	High oxygen demand, therefore increases BOD, reduced DO, reduced primary production, therefore reduced chlorophyll.	DO chlorophyll BOD
Total nitrates	High levels will promote primary production. May be created by the oxidation of ammonia. It is a primary sewage indicator/index.	coliforms
Total phosphates	Sewage produces high levels of phosphates and it is therefore connected with faecal coliforms.	chlorophyll faecal coliforms
Total coliforms	Original micro-biological indicator. Can be naturally occurring.	BOD
Thermo-tolerant faecal coliforms	More specific sub-group of above. *Salmonella* is highly correlated with high levels.	*Salmonella*
E.coli	Thought to be a good micro-biological indicator of sewage effluent but levels are typically low.	BOD phosphates
Turbidity	Strongly related to parameters such as sediment load, effluent.	sediment chlorophyll
Surface film (oil and foam)	Included, as surface films of whatever nature will have a strong effect on the reflectance of the water.	

above the water's surface, clear of obstruction, by a tripod and 2 m boom arrangement. This could be swung round to record from a spectral reference panel. Data were recorded throughout a 4 h period, 2 h either side of high or low tide. Water samples were taken 2 h before, 2 h after, and at high/low tide. This was carried out for a month in late summer (22 August–22 September).

The spectral data were collected using the normal scan mode with three gratings through the range 0.3–1.0 μm at a resolution of 2 nm, 1.0–1.8 μm at 4 nm and

1.8–2.5 μm at 5 nm. Instruments such as CASI offer ranges within this and similar resolutions e.g. 1.8 nm and range 0.4–0.9 μm. One waveband of interest would certainly have been within the thermal infrared, but much is already known about temperature measurement and thus, the limitation of the spectral range was not considered to be a problem.

RESULTS AND ANALYSIS OF SPECTRAL DATA FOR EACH PARAMETER

This period of field work has resulted in the collection of around 100 sets of water quality data and 750 sets of spectral data. The spectral data have now been processed, but some laboratory work is still being completed. The initial direction of the data analysis has been to uncover any correlations or relationships between the selected water quality parameters, including tidal state and weather conditions. These relationships have been used to assist in the calculation of the estimated water quality data for spectral readings with incomplete water truth data. This has produced over 700 sets of spectral recordings with corresponding water quality data. Graphical software has been written to analyse the spectral signatures of the water in an effort to simplify the data initially. This software allows the 'tagging' of spectral signatures to match key spectral reflectance curves such as those illustrated in Figure 2. Other early stages of the analysis will determine whether there are any straightforward correlations between the parameters and the wavelengths recorded. Few results had been completed by December 1995 as the software was still under development and data were still under initial analysis. The sample parameters being used for this developmental stage of the research are the micro-biological parameters (total coliform, faecal coliform and *E.coli*) which have shown some relationship within the range 390-700 nm. This is illustrated in Figure 2.

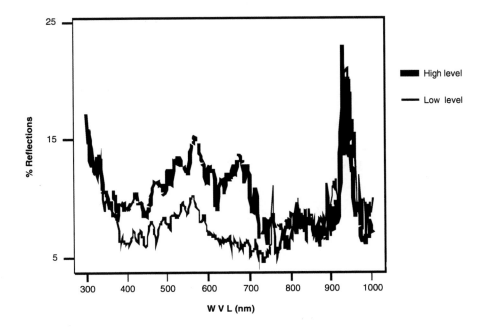

Figure 2. Example of the reflectance of the study area with high or low levels of microbiological parameters (*E.coli*, faecal coliform, total coliform)

SUMMARY

In the longer term, thorough statistical analysis of the spectral data in relation to the water quality parameters will be carried out to search for time-lagged relationships, ratios, and multiple variable relationships. It is expected to take up to a year before this analysis can produce any true results.

REFERENCES

Baban, S. (1993) Detecting water quality parameters in the Norfolk Broads, UK using Landsat Imagery. *International Journal of Remote Sensing*, **14**(7): 1247-1267.

Chacon Torres, A., Ross, L.C., Beveridge, M.C.M. and Watson, A.I. (1992) The application of spot multispectral imagery for the assessment of water quality in the Lake Patzcuaro, Mexico. *International Journal of Remote Sensing*, **13**(4): 587-603.

Clark, C. (1993) Satellite remote sensing for marine pollution investigations. *Marine Pollution Bulletin*, **26**(7): 357-368.

Dekker, A. and Peters, S. (1993) The use of Thematic Mapper for the analysis of eutrophic lakes: a case study in the Netherlands. *International Journal of Remote Sensing*, **14**(5): 799-821.

Forster, B., Xingwei, S. and Baide, X. (1993) Remote sensing of sea water quality parameters using Landsat TM. *International Journal of Remote Sensing*, **14**(15): 2759-2771.

Friedrich, W. (1991) The use of remote sensing in coastal research. *Geojournal*, **24**(1): 71-76.

Gitelson, A., Garbuzov, G., Szilagyi, F., Mittenzwey, K.H., Karnieli, A. and Kaiser, A. (1993) Quantitative remote sensing methods for real time monitoring of inland waters quality. *International Journal of Remote Sensing*, **14**(7): 1269-1295.

Gunter, G. (1991) Remote sensing in inter-governmental programmes of ocean research and monitoring. *Geojournal*, **24**(1): 67-69.

Harper, B. and Curtis, M. (1993) Coastal zone mapping. *Mapping Awareness and GIS in Europe*, **7**(1): 17-20.

Johnson, S. and Corcelle, G. (1989) *The Environmental Policy of the European Communities*. Graham and I Trotman.

Kay, D. (1992) *Recreational Water Quality Management (Coastal Waters)*. Ellis Horwood Ltd.

Laws, E.A. (1993) *Aquatic Pollution, an Introductory Text*, 2nd edn. Chichester: John Wiley and Sons.

Lillesand, T.M. and Kiefer, R.W. (1987) *Remote Sensing and Image Interpretation*, 2nd edn. Chichester: John Wiley and Sons.

Matthews, A. and Boxall, S. (1994) Novel algorithms for the determination of phytoplankton concentration and maturity. Presented at the *Second Thematic Conference on Remote Sensing for Marine and Coastal Environments, New Orleans, Louisiana*.

Open University (1978) *Oceanography Chemical Processes*. Milton Keynes: The Open University.

Pattiaratchi, C., Lavery, P., Weyyllie, A. and Hick, P. (1994) Estimates of water quality in coastal waters using multi-date Landsat Thematic Mapper data. *International Journal of Remote Sensing*, **15**(8): 1571-1584.

Roberts, A. (1994) Multisensor remote sensing of water quality in Spit Lake, Manitoba. Presented at the *Forty-Third Scottish Summer School in Physics, 1-16 August 1994*.

Tebbutt, T.H.Y. (1992) *Principles of Water Pollution Control, 4th edn*. Pergammon Press.

Thomann, R.V. and Mueller, J.A. (1987) *Principles of Surface Water Quality Modelling and Control*. Harper Collins Publishers Inc.

Application of Remote Sensing and GIS for Monitoring Vegetation in Etosha National Park

C. Sannier[1], J. C. Taylor[1], W. du Plessis[2] and K. Campbell[3]

[1]Cranfield University, School of Agriculture, Food and Environment, Silsoe, Bedford, MK45 4DT, UK.

[2]Etosha Ecological Institute, PO Okaukuejo, via Outjo, Namibia.

[3]Natural Resources Institute, Chatham Maritime, Chatham, Kent, ME4 4TB, UK.

ABSTRACT

The monitoring of vegetation in Etosha National Park, Namibia, is essential if the interactions between the wildlife population, the possibility of climate change, and the vegetation resources, are to be understood. Such an understanding is necessary for establishing management strategies to ensure that the Park is sustainable as an important unit for the conservation of wildlife and for tourism. This study aims to produce maps of vegetation status in near real time from NOAA images acquired from the local LARST receiving station. In order to assess vegetation status, map products based on the NDVI need to be put into historical context and stratified to remove the effects of the different vegetation types. A classification scheme for the Etosha vegetation, based mainly on the dominant species composition and the physiognomy of the woody component, has been designed. A combination of field measurements and analysis of Landsat TM imagery has provided a stratification of the Park. Historical data were extracted from the ARTEMIS NDVI GAC archive and processed to obtain, in combination with the stratification, standard NDVI profiles for each of the main types of vegetation. These are related to the LAC NDVI data obtained in real time from the receiving station to derive a vegetation status map for each 10-day period.

BACKGROUND

The monitoring of vegetation in the 22 300 km^2 Etosha National Park, Namibia, is essential if the interactions between the wildlife population, the possibility of climate change, and the vegetation resources, are to be understood. Such an understanding is necessary for establishing management strategies whch ensure that the Park is sustainable as an important unit for the conservation of wildlife and for tourism.

Relating vegetation conditions to rainfall is one way of monitoring vegetation. However, the climate in Etosha is semi-arid with a highly variable, temporal and spatial distribution of rainfall, and the existing network of rain gauges is not dense enough to allow for this approach. Satellite images provide complete coverage of the Park from which map products can be derived.

A receiving station was installed in Etosha Ecological Institute by the LARST project (Williams and Rosenberg, 1993) to acquire NOAA-AVHRR images. These are usually processed to produce maps showing the spatial variation in terms of the NDVI (Normalized Difference Vegetation Index) which is related to the vegetation greeness. However, NDVI images are not easily interpretable by users. The objective of this study is to derive a product which overcomes this problem.

NDVI TIME RESPONSE OF DIFFERENT VEGETATION TYPES

NDVI image maps are difficult to interpret, firstly, because an explicit relationship between NDVI and vegetation condition is not available and secondly, because there may be different relationships for each vegetation type.

The FAO-ARTEMIS (Africa Real Time Environmental Monitoring Information System) NOAA AVHRR NDVI image bank was used to investigate the influence of vegetation type on the NDVI. The data consist of an archive of GAC (Global Area Coverage) 10-day maximum value composite images at 7.6 km resolution covering the whole of the African continent from August 1981 to June 1991.

Figure 1 shows the 10 year averaged values of NDVI for each 10-day period over the season for some locations in Etosha with different known cover types. The NDVI over High Tree Savanna is systematically higher than that for Shrub Savanna, which is systematically higher than that for Grassland. This established the need to stratify the Park into the main vegetation types.

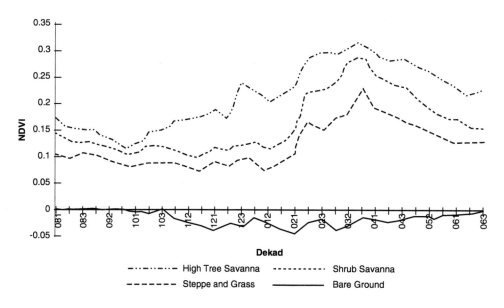

Figure 1. Average profile of four land cover types from the ARTEMIS archive

CLASSIFICATION OF ETOSHA NATIONAL PARK FOR STRATIFICATION INTO THE MAIN VEGETATION TYPES

A classification scheme was developed following the philosophy described by Boughey (1957). It was adapted to the semi-arid conditions of Etosha and was based primarily on physiognomic characteristics of the woody vegetation component. Figure 2 shows the decision tree which was produced to assist the field data collection. The dominant tree species were also recorded.

There was a need for an unbiased method of collecting field data to enable classification errors to be measured objectively. This was adapted from that described by Taylor and Eva (1992). The vegetation types were mapped in a randomly aligned systematic sample of 1 km square areas. In all, 220 sites were selected over the whole Park but only 173 of them were surveyed because 47 were situated on the salt pan where the cover was known.

Survey documents were produced to assist the field mapping. Landsat TM imagery was geometrically corrected, with an RMS error better than 30 m, using the UTM (Universal Transverse Mercator) projection. This allowed the whole Park to be covered with a single co-ordinate system which was also available on most GPS (Global Positioning System) receivers. All the 173 sites were surveyed by air, navigating by the GPS. A video recording of each site was made to facilitate checking. Some sites were also surveyed on the ground in order to calibrate and check the interpretation from the air.

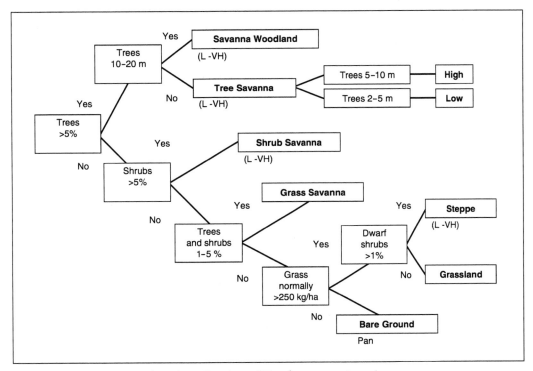

Figure 2. Decision tree for identification of Etosha vegetation classes

The data collected were entered into a database and a sub-set was used to train the maximum likelihood classifier. The supervised classification was performed using 33 classes grouped into four categories: bare ground (pan), grassland (and steppe), shrub savanna and tree savanna. For these broad classes, the overall agreement of the vegetation map with ground observations was estimated to be 89%.

TIME SERIES ANALYSIS OF NDVI FOR STATUS CRITERIA

The vegetation classification of Etosha allows the time-series NDVI profiles to be extracted for each vegetation type.

The probability distribution of the NDVI was calculated for each 10-day period during the growing season. This was achieved by applying a methodology similar to that used for assessing the probability of extreme hydrological events (Linsley *et al.*, 1975). The analysis was used to define quintile ranges of NDVI for each vegetation class and each 10-day period. Five classes were chosen as defined in Table 1. Figure 3 shows the flow chart corresponding to the described processes.

Table 1. Definition of vegetation status classes

Probability of a lower NDVI (%)	Vegetation status
<20	Very poor
20 to 39	Poor
40 to 59	Normal
60 to 79	Good
≥80	Very good

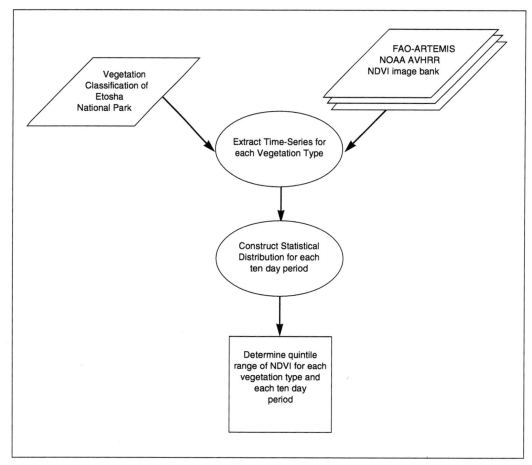

Figure 3. Time series analysis of NDVI for status criteria

PRODUCTION OF STATUS MAPS FOR CURRENT IMAGES

A number of NOAA-AVHRR LAC images acquired at the local receiving station in Etosha National Park during the last rainy season were used. The images were geo-referenced to the vegetation map of the Park. Final RMS errors were between 0.5 and 0.9 pixel. The LAC images were resampled using cubic convolution and a 500 m output pixel size. This was to preserve maximum spatial detail.

The AVHRR channels 1 and 2 were radiometrically corrected using the method described by Kaufman and Holben (1993). NDVI images were computed, and a further correction was applied to remove atmospheric noise by using part of the Etosha pan as a standard target. The same correction was also applied to the ARTEMIS data so that NDVI values computed from each source were compatible.

The status maps were produced as illustrated in Figure 4. The vegetation type of the LAC pixel was determined by reference to the vegetation map. The NDVI value at that location was then compared with the status criteria for the vegetation type at that time and assigned to the appropriate status class. This process was repeated for the whole image, producing the vegetation status map for the period considered.

CONCLUSIONS AND FURTHER DEVELOPMENTS

This study is still on-going but some useful conclusions can already be drawn:

- a cost-effective methodology for vegetation mapping in Africa, using satellite imagery and a statistically designed field survey for calibration and validation, has been demonstrated;
- as the vegetation status maps could be produced using data collected from the low-cost LARST receiving stations and the FAO-ARTEMIS archive, the methodology is potentially applicable to other countries in Africa.

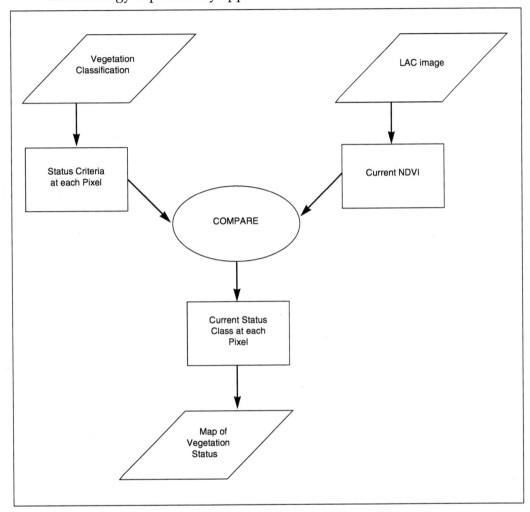

Figure 4. Production of status maps

The status maps from the 1995 rainy season appear to relate very well to the actual conditions on the ground. However, there is a need for a more formal assessment of the status maps, for which work is on-going. A similar product is being developed, based on the cumulative NDVI, which will assess the vegetation conditions for a whole season. The methodology will be tested operationally in the next rainy season at the Etosha Ecological Institute.

REFERENCES

Boughey, A.S. (1957) The physiognomic delimitation of West African vegetation types. *Journal of the West African Science Association*, **3**(2): 148-165.

Kaufman, Y.J. and Holben, B.N. (1993) Calibration of the AVHHR visible and near-IR bands by atmospheric scattering, ocean glint and desert reflection. *International Journal of Remote Sensing*, **14**(1): 21-52.

Linsley, R.K., Kohler, M.A. and Paulhus, J.H. (1975) Probability in hydrology: a basis for design. pp. 338-372. In: *Hydrology for Engineers*. Mac Graham Hill.

Taylor, J.C. and Eva, H.D. (1992) *Regional Inventories on Beds, Cambs and Northants (UK)*. Final Report. Contract NO. 4817-92-06 ED ISP GB Joint Research Centre, Commission of the European Communities. Silsoe College, Silsoe.

Williams, J.B. and Rosenberg, L.J. (1993) Operational reception, processing and application of satellite data in developing countries : theory and practice. pp. 76-81. In: Hilton, K. (ed.), *Towards Operational Applications. Proceedings, 19th Annual Conference of the Remote Sensing Society.*

The Development of GIS and Remote Sensing Techniques in the Centre for Arid Zone Studies, North East Nigeria

A. C. Bird[1], N. D. Pratt[1], and A. I. Lawan[2]

[1]Silsoe College, Cranfield University, Silsoe, Beds, MK45 4DT, UK.
[2]Centre for Arid Zone Studies, University of Maiduguri, Maiduguri, Nigeria.

ABSTRACT

The Centre for Arid Zone Studies (CAZS) acts as a focus within the University of Maiduguri for multi-disciplinary research and training in support of arid zone development. An important element of this support is the provision of Image Processing (IP) and Geographic Information System (GIS) facilities for the storage, processing and analysis of satellite imagery, thematic maps and other spatial data. This facility has been developed over the past five years with assistance from Silsoe College, Cranfield University, and funding from the European Union. Equipment has been installed, and training carried out, at PhD., MSc. and technical level, with staff from many departments in the University. In addition to the computer-based GIS and image processing techniques, field work has formed an important element of this training. The approach has been to work alongside local staff and assist them in developing the skills and experience directly relevant to their environment. The main theme of the remote sensing applications has been land use and land cover mapping for an area which is the subject of a major sustainable development programme. A SPOT and Landsat-based study has produced results on general land cover and land use, while a separate SPOT study has investigated the estimation of areas under irrigation. Both projects have evaluated the role of satellite imagery in the provision of the information needed to guide the management of the area's natural resources.

INTRODUCTION

The North East Arid Zone Development Programme (NEAZDP), funded jointly by the European Development Fund and the Federal Government of Nigeria, was established in 1990 in northern Borno State with the aim of raising living standards in the region by stimulating sustainable rural economic development. The programme has co-ordinated major developments in rural infrastructure, water supplies, education and health care.

As a response to the regional environmental and economic problems which resulted from drought in the 1970s and 1980s, the Centre for Arid Zone Studies (CAZS) was established at the University of Maiduguri with a Government mandate to carry out research into the environmental and economic problems facing Nigeria's drier regions. In formulating NEAZDP, it was recognized that such an ambitious programme would require a research input, and that this would most appropriately be provided by an indigenous institution. A major portion of the NEAZDP financing agreement was therefore allocated to CAZS to facilitate a programme of supportive research. This was intended to serve the dual purpose of providing answers to NEAZDP and strengthening CAZS, and in so doing, to ensure it's long-term sustainability as a regional support centre. To support CAZS in this role, a link programme was established with Silsoe College. The aim was to strengthen CAZS in terms of it's manpower and research capability. This has been met through a programme of research and a programme of staff development addressing problems in Water Resources, Crop and Livestock Production, Soil and Water Management, Socio-Economics and Environment and Resource Monitoring.

At the beginning of the linkage, researchers at the University of Maiduguri and personnel at NEAZDP were aware of the lack of currently available information on the infrastructure and land resources of the development programme area. The utility of existing mapped information was limited. Settlement and land use patterns had changed, quite dramatically in places, since the publication of the most recent 1:50 000 scale topographic maps. The mapping of settlement locations and names was found to be unreliable. This deficiency in basic information was recognized as a major constraint to effective prioritization, targeting, and allocation of development initiatives. It was also recognized that remotely sensed data, including digital analysis of satellite imagery, had potential for filling certain aspects of this data gap. Other data would be gained by socio-economic surveys conducted by NEAZDP and CAZS. The analytical capabilities of GIS were recognized as holding great potential for the incorporation of land resource data derived from remote sensing, and other diverse data, into a single data analysis framework. The starting point for developing the applications of remote sensing and GIS was the establishment of a digital data processing facility in CAZS.

HARDWARE AND SOFTWARE

A combination of PC-based hardware and software was installed which combined low cost and ease of use with good functionality. The process of installing the hardware and software in a university with no previous experience of digital image processing and GIS, led to the consideration of the following factors: hardware availability, hardware maintenance, working environment, hardware and software appropriateness, cost and training (Falloux *et al.*, 1991). It was also necessary to provide air-conditioning, dust-proofing, an uninterruptable power supply, a diesel generator and room security devices.

Image processing and GIS functions were provided by the software package known as ILWIS (Integrated Land and Water Information System). This package has been under development by ITC Enschede in the Netherlands since 1986 (Valenzuela, 1988). ILWIS provides a series of functions which allow the input and analysis of vector maps, raster maps, raster images and database tables. The user interacts with the software *via* a series of menus which require the keying in of answers to questions. A major advantage of this package is that it combines all the essential IP and GIS functions under the same operating system and the same menu structure, thus simplifying the training process.

The hardware in the facility consisted of a 486 33 MHz PC with a 300 Mb hard disk, an external tape streamer, mono and colour monitors, an A1 digitizing table, an A3 colour raster inkjet printer, a wide carriage dot matrix printer, an uninterruptable power supply, an air conditioning unit and a diesel generator.

Hardware items were purchased in Nigeria and initially covered by maintenance contracts with the supplier. In addition to this, a contractor was identified in Maiduguri who was capable of carrying out electrical and hardware repairs. This greatly aided the viability of the facility.

PERSONNEL AND TRAINING

The training and development of staff was central to the work carried out in remote sensing and GIS, given that useful results could only be obtained from this technology if it was correctly applied. Training took place at Silsoe College and the University of Maiduguri. The user group for the facility included members of staff from the Departments of Biological Sciences, Civil and Water Resources Engineering, Computer Sciences, Crop Science, Geography, Geology and Soil Sciences. A member of Silsoe staff worked at the University as a GIS specialist for four years. Several approaches were used to provide training and raise awareness for staff at different levels.

Two members of staff from the Department of Geography were selected for postgraduate training at Silsoe in applied remote sensing and GIS. Their work was carried out on the same combination of hardware and software as that at CAZS. One carried out research on the application of image analysis within a GIS for monitoring land cover changes (Abdalla, 1994). The other investigated the application of high resolution satellite imagery for land use and land cover mapping in the hope that this would provide an important input to the design of future monitoring techniques for the NEAZDP area.

Another member of staff from the Biological Sciences Department carried out a three-month professional development period at Silsoe, during which he was trained in remote sensing and GIS. This prepared him for work in a desertification research project.

The operation of the facility required a team of technical staff who could be responsible for inputting data, managing the PC and peripherals, and assisting with data processing. Two technicians with specialisms in cartography and surveying were seconded on a part-time basis to work for CAZS in the IP/GIS facility. They were trained in digitizing and data processing by the resident Silsoe specialist and attended a computing course in Maiduguri.

PROMOTING APPLICATIONS

In order to realize the full potential, it was felt necessary to generate enough academic understanding and interest within the university, in addition to good technical staff, to support research projects requiring the use of image processing and GIS technology. To encourage this, a two-week workshop was held in October 1993; 15 academic staff from seven university departments, the local Polytechnic, NEAZDP and the Nguru/Hadeija Wetlands Project, participated in the workshop. It provided a mixture of theoretical and practical training in remote sensing and GIS, and included a field visit to the NEAZDP project area. The aim was to introduce people to the subject, make them aware of the contribution the technology could make to their own research, and help them formulate short projects which could be executed as a focus for further training. This helped to develop an enthusiastic core group of users who were keen to build on this knowledge and use the CAZS facility. It also encouraged a multi-disciplinary approach with members of different departments working together.

APPLICATIONS

The application projects initiated during the linkage between Silsoe and the University of Maiduguri were aimed at supporting the development work carried out by NEAZDP. The role for GIS in storing and presenting spatial data about the programme area was developed. This included the digitizing of overlays to aerial photograph mosaics, the digitizing of map information, and the analysing and printing of maps for field work and reports. Satellite imagery of sections of the programme area were obtained from the Landsat MSS, Landsat TM, SPOT Multispectral and SPOT Panchromatic sensors. The mapping of land cover using satellite imagery was studied in both PhD. and MSc. projects.

Three major research projects were initiated at CAZS to take advantage of the availability of satellite imagery linked to the potential for site visits to collect essential ground data.

Land and Water Resources Information Database
This was a demonstration project, carried out in close co-operation with NEAZDP, for building a database of spatial data from a variety of sources to

assist in planning activities. It formed the starting point for the development of GIS facilities at the NEAZDP headquarters.

Agricultural Statistics

Field survey work was carried out on a sample basis to determine the feasibility of following the approach currently employed in Europe for estimating crop areas. This is described in more detail in a later section.

Survey of Forest Resources and Land Degradation

In this project, current and historic aerial photographs, satellite imagery, and current field work were used to assess land degradation in the NEAZDP area. An important element of this project was the training of a team of interpreters to work consistently on the classification of the region.

EXTENDING THE TECHNOLOGY TO NEAZDP

The work carried out on the GIS/IP facility was designed with the data processing and research interests of both CAZS and NEAZDP in mind. Each project was discussed with the relevant NEAZDP staff, and training sessions were open to CAZS and NEAZDP people. CAZS provided image processing and GIS facilities to a temporary NEAZDP worker studying forest and grazing reserve encroachment trends. CAZS facilities were used for digitizing a 1:250 000 scale land use map of the NEAZDP area, in order to provide area calculations and assist in the digitizing of a series of NEAZDP area management maps. NEAZDP subsequently elected to purchase identical software to CAZS in order to develop its own IP/GIS and to work in parallel with CAZS.

LAND COVER MAPPING

A PhD. project compared SPOT XS and Landsat TM imagery in terms of their effectiveness for land use and land cover mapping and inventory. A central element of this work was a field survey carried out over a full 12 month period. This allowed the researcher to develop an appropriate classification scheme and monitor the changes in land cover which occurred as the seasons changed. The final classification of the imagery was based on the six class scheme of water, woodland, agro/pastoral land, floodplain irrigation, wetland vegetation and developed land. An overall accuracy of 65% was achieved. The field data were combined with the classifications to make area estimates for each class.

A further issue addressed by the field work was the collection of suitable ground control data for geometric correction of imagery. Problems arose with the geometric correction of satellite imagery in areas where suitable topographic maps were not available. Global Positioning System (GPS) technology was seen as a potential solution. This aspect of the study was extended, in terms of satellite imagery, to the geometric correction of Landsat MSS (80 m pixel), Landsat TM (30 m pixel), and SPOT Panchromatic (10 m pixel) satellite images. Corrections were carried out using 1:100 000 scale topographic maps and GPS data collected during the land cover field survey. Geometric corrections with first degree polynomials, using either GPS derived points or 1:100 000 scale topographic map derived points, yielded RMS error values in the order of ± 35 m for all three types of satellite image, regardless of pixel size (Kardoulas *et al.*, in press).

AGRICULTURAL STATISTICS

Monitoring agriculture using remote sensing techniques is now becoming an operational technology in Europe (Meyer-Roux and Vossen, 1994). The approach depends on a combination of field work and image processing for calculating the areas of land cultivated with certain crops. Such procedures have to be adapted for use in northern Nigeria where the logistics of the field survey are more complex, and data have to be collected at several different times during the year in order to cover the different crops which follow the seasons. One element of this was tested by the project.

In January 1994, a SPOT XS image was collected for a test area at a time when a field team was carrying out a mapping exercise for irrigated vegetables. As the basis for estimating the area of irrigated land at that time 80, 500 x 500 m sample squares were being mapped. As a result, SPOT XS imagery, and ground data in the form of an area-frame sample, were collected simultaneously. The aim of the survey was to test a methodology for providing area estimates of land under small-scale irrigation in the complex floodplain terrain which forms an important part of the NEAZDP area. The long-term contribution of the work was to assist in the planning and costing of operational exercises to provide timely agricultural data for the local planners.

The classification of the satellite imagery produced low mapping accuracies, and the area estimated from pixel counts was highly dependent on the classification procedure. The combination of the image and field data to allow the use of the regression estimator approach provided much more consistent measurements of area (Taylor and Eva, 1993). Although the confidence intervals on these results were relatively wide (e.g. 788 ± 319 ha in an area of 25 250 ha), there is no alternative source of information for planners in the study area. The analysis revealed that the level of field work would have to be increased by a factor of 4 to gain comparable confidence intervals from ground survey alone.

CONCLUSIONS

The work described in this paper has been carried out in the context of an EC funded linkage between the University of Maiduguri, Nigeria, and Silsoe College, Cranfield University, UK. The short-term success of this project has been based around three essential items. First, funding was available for both equipment and satellite imagery at the start of the linkage and this was used to purchase low-cost, robust equipment which could be maintained locally. Secondly, a member of Silsoe's staff was based at the University of Maiduguri for four years; this allowed the creation of training material based entirely on local data, and the development of close working relationships with many members of staff. Thirdly, staff at many levels in the University were involved in the work, as were staff from supporting or associated organizations. This allowed a core of people with skills, knowledge and enthusiasm to be gradually assembled. The long-term success of the project will depend on these people and their ability to attract funds for further work.

REFERENCES

Abdalla, J.D. (1994) *The Evaluation of Satellite Imagery in a Geographic Information System (GIS) for Monitoring Land Cover Changes in a Semi-Arid Area of North-Eastern Nigeria*. PhD. thesis [unpublished], Silsoe College, Cranfield University, UK.

Falloux, F., O'Brien, C. and van Genderen, J.L. (1991) Environmental information systems for renewable resource management in sub-Saharan Africa: issues. pp. 323-332. In: *Proceedings of the Second European Conference on GIS Brussels*.

Kardoulas, N.G., Bird, A.C. and Lawan, A.I. (in press) Geometric correction of SPOT and Landsat imagery: a comparison of map and GPS derived control points. *Photogrammetric Engineering and Remote Sensing*.

Meyer-Roux, J. and Vossen, P. (1994) The first phase of the MARS project, 1988-1993: overview, methods and results. pp. 33-81. In: *Proceedings of the Conference on the MARS Project: Overview and Perspectives, Belgirate, Italy, 1993.* Luxembourg: Publication EUR 15599 EN of the Office for Official Publications of the European Communities.

Taylor, J.C. and Eva, H.D. (1993) Operational use of remote sensing for estimating crop areas in England. In: *Towards Operational Applications. Proceedings of the 19th Annual Conference of the Remote Sensing Society, Chester, UK, 1993.* Nottingham: Remote Sensing Society.

Valenzuela, C.R. (1988) 'ILWIS Overview', *ITC Journal*, 1988-1. Enschede, The Netherlands.

Environmental Impact Assessment of Tsetse Control: Methodology for the Historical Quantification of Land Cover and Land Use

Alan Mills and Judith Pender

Natural Resources Institute, Central Avenue, Chatham Maritime, Chatham, Kent ME4 4TB, UK.

ABSTRACT

Tsetse flies are a major constraint to livestock production in tropical Africa through their transmission of animal trypanosomiasis. Control of tsetse has been the primary method of reducing trypanosomiasis in Zimbabwe for more than 50 years. In north-western Zimbabwe near Lake Kariba, the limit of fly distribution has been pushed northwards since 1980 by successive campaigns using a variety of control methods. An EIA of this area is assessing the effect of control on the changing pattern of land use since 1972. GIS layers of land use and land cover have been extracted from Landsat imagery to gain baseline data for the study. Patterns of land use and vegetation types are immediately apparent from a false colour composite Landsat image. Land cover was determined using 1993 dry season Landsat Thematic Mapper data in combination with over 200 field sites taken in the wet and dry seasons of 1993. Substrate variation in the area interfered with image classification. The image was divided into three by applying masks defined in band 7 and relating to light, medium and dark substrate reflectances. The division helped visual definition of training sites as well as minimizing confusion between similar cover types on different substrates. A maximum likelihood algorithm was used to classify the masked images in bands 2, 3 and 4 and the resulting classified images rejoined. TWINSPAN cluster analysis was applied to the field data in order to provide confidence in the classification. Landsat imagery between 1972 and 1993 has been used to quantify HDLU changes by equating human dominated land use (HDLU) with bare fields in dry season imagery. A Sobel filter of Band 7 assisted in the definition of areas of HDLU. Light tones were indicative of areas representing recently harvested cultivation, transport infrastructure and buildings. These areas were further highlighted by edge enhancement. Areas of HDLU could then be digitized as ARC/INFO format polygons. HDLU data were integrated into the GIS with information on land cover type, geology, proximity to roads and tsetse spray history, for further analysis.

Using GIS and Satellite Imagery to Determine Potential Areas within the Thames Chase Community Forest for Initial Implementation of Strategy

David Bolsdon and Simon Evans

Anglia Polytechnic University, Victoria Road South, Chelmsford, Essex, CM1 1LL, UK.

ABSTRACT

The Community Forest initiative was launched in 1989 as a joint venture between the Countryside and Forestry Commissions. Twelve areas have been designated, each sharing predominantly urban fringe locations. Such areas tend to suffer problems associated with land use pressures and are often characterized by a negative image and a concomitant lack of investment potential. The Community Forest initiative aims to improve local environments in line with the principles of sustainable development, advocating an approach of creating an improved woodland environment in order to spur social and economic regeneration. This paper focuses on the Thames Chase Community Forest which is situated to the east of London and which comprises a range of land quality zones determined by land use and associated pressures. Issues are considered which relate to policy objectives and regenerative priority in the initial implementation of Community Forest strategy, and the extent to which they interact. The satellite imagery used was derived from the Institute of Terrestrial Ecology's Land Cover Map of Great Britain. Other data sources included Agricultural Land Classification data from the Ministry of Agriculture Fisheries and Food (MAFF) and mineral activity data derived from the Thames Chase Community Forest plan. The methods used combined remote sensing and geographic information systems (GIS) techniques. This allowed the production of enhanced spatial and analytical queries and the provision of information for comparison across a range of environments.

INTRODUCTION

The aim of this paper is to describe the methods used to devise a methodology for determining the initial priorities for implementing the Thames Chase Community Forest initiative. The introduction of national policies, aimed at the expansion of forestry development to satisfy multiple objectives, signals a new approach towards planning and managing the forest resource. Policies reflect the dynamic nature of land use and forest related demands, and the increased opportunities associated with lowland expansion are indicative of the need to reduce agricultural production. An important area identified as a priority for lowland expansion is the urban fringe, a zone which suffers a variety of accredited problems associated with its proximity to urban centres. Existing land character and use within Community Forest project areas has been identified from a number of disparate sources, which reduces the effectiveness of comparative assessment between and within individual project areas. The methods chosen for this research allow the integration of existing remotely sensed data with enhanced spatial information which can be analysed within a GIS. This allows standardization of the information considered vital for determining a priority focus for implementation.

THE COMMUNITY FOREST CONCEPT

Although the Community Forest initiative covers a range of environments along the urban to rural gradient, it is essentially focused on the zone of transition between the two called the urban fringe. The initiative is designed as a multi-purpose development encompassing a broad range of nationally stated objectives which relate to issues such as recreational provision, landscape improvement, conservation and education. However, the ultimate aims are the regeneration of urban fringe environments, the improvement of image and the attraction of sufficient investment to sustain beneficial change. This paper concentrates on the latter aim while recognizing that it is the interaction of all potential benefits which will determine the overall success of the initiative.

THAMES CHASE

The Community Forest initiative currently includes 12 designated project areas located around towns and cities in England. Thames Chase is situated to the east of London and covers an area of about 98 420 km^2 of urban fringe land. It is characterized by a mosaic of land uses in close juxtaposition to major population centres. To the north of the project area, the landscape is already well wooded and valued for its landscape quality; the south, however, is characterized by poor environments and has been the subject of significant mineral extraction. Although the predominant land use is agriculture, land holdings tend to be marginal enterprises lacking an existing woodland structure. This has implications for the image of the area as it is clearly visible to the major transport corridors which bisect it. Development is restricted by the inclusion of the area within the Metropolitan Green Belt (MGB), so environmental upgrading is viewed as an important strategic consideration.

MECHANISMS FOR CHANGE

As the development of the Community Forest initiative does not involve public acquisition of land, project teams are dependent on negotiation and persuasion as their main instruments of implementation. Several grant aid incentives are available for landowners who agree to diversify into forestry related enterprises, and payment levels reflect the need to aim initial planting schemes towards priority areas.

Woodland Grant Scheme (WGS)

The main incentive for developing forestry land use is the Woodland Grant Scheme (WGS), operated by the Forestry Commission, which encourages the establishment and management of woodlands and forests nationwide. The increased payments for broadleaved planting reflect the multi-purpose benefits associated with this form of development, and supplements are available to encourage forestry development in areas of priority such as the Community Forests.

The supplements to the WGS are:

- Community Woodland Supplement
- Better Land Supplement
- Locational Allowance

The Community Woodland Supplement is for the provision of access and recreation to local communities and is available to landowners operating within 8 km of a built-up area. It is specifically targeted at the establishment of new woodlands. The Better Land Supplement reflects the need to curb agricultural output in the light of the significant surplus production across the European Community. Forestry development has been identified as a key diversification approach, and extra payments are available for landowners to establish woodlands on land currently under arable crops, and for areas of improved grassland. The Locational Allowance has recently been introduced to increase the levels of new planting in key areas such as the Community Forests and the National Forest.

Agricultural Grants

The Farm Woodland Premium Scheme (FWPS) offers annual payments to farmers establishing new woodlands. It is one of a range of measures introduced to promote forestry development as an alternative to agriculture. Other incentives include Set Aside, Countryside Premium and Hedgerow Incentive Schemes, and a range of grants available from local authorities and other organizations such as the Woodland Trust. Initially, high quality agricultural land (Grades 1 and 2) will be unlikely to be included extensively in farmers' planting schemes because of the value of the land and the need to prevent land sterilization by irreversible development. The more marginal farmland is most likely to contribute to the Community Forests in the initial implementation period and as such, this land has been considered a priority.

Derelict Land Grant (DLG)

Further areas for priority planting are those damaged by mineral extraction activities. The southern part of Thames Chase contains significant areas of land degraded or derelict as a result of previous practices. As environmental issues are being increasingly translated into policy, current grant aid structures recommend the restoration of land to soft end uses in general, with forestry providing a key contribution to environmental and landscape improvement. The strict geographical limits of dereliction in Thames Chase precludes the application of a rolling programme for DLG payments. This reduces the effectiveness of policy in areas where mining dereliction is not considered to be of regional importance. In this respect, the range of agricultural grants is expected to prove more attractive to participants in implementing Thames Chase strategy, and they therefore assume enhanced policy priority.

Other Priority Areas

This paper considers Community Forest implementation in terms of spurring the environmental and landscape improvements required for upgrading the image of the area, and the subsequent economic and social benefits that these are expected to achieve. Further areas of priority will include the periphery of transport networks for visual screening and ambient noise reduction. The extension of existing woodland units is considered to be important because of their role in enhancing wildlife corridors, although in some areas, the designation of conservation zones (e.g. SSSI) may preclude new plantings.

Areas of priority utilized in developing the methodology therefore relate to:

- agricultural land (especially Grades 3–5);
- areas in close proximity to centres of population;
- degraded and derelict land; and
- land alongside transport networks.

DATA SOURCES

The data for the preliminary investigations came from a wide variety of sources. Some came directly *via* the Internet using the File Transfer Protocol (FTP) and others were captured manually using a digitizing table and paper maps. The coverages (data layers) include physical and non-physical features, with each coverage relating to a different phenomenon. The methods used for data capture, and the conversion of the spatial and attribute data, are discussed below.

Land Cover

One of the most important coverages used in the study was the Land Cover dataset. This was derived from the Institute of Terrestrial Ecology's (ITE) Land Cover Map of Great Britain. The map was produced between 1988 and 1991 using cloud-free images from the American Landsat satellite. The on-board sensor (Thematic Mapper) recorded the reflected solar radiation in seven wavebands of the spectrum from ground cells approximately 30 m across. The Landsat satellite completes a coverage of the whole of the earth's surface every 16 days. For the production of the map, summer and winter satellite images were combined to enhance the seasonal differences in the various land cover types. Although urban areas have a similar reflectance value all year round, deciduous woodland has a different reflectance when the trees have shed their foliage than when they are in leaf. Arable land also changes from bare ground to being covered with plant growth as the annual cycle is completed.

The scenes were supplied to the ITE as 185 km squares and were then geometrically registered to the British National Grid. An output grid cell size of 25 m^2 was decided upon by the ITE, to retain the original resolution with a more convenient grid size. An image of the combined summer and winter data was displayed on a visual display unit (VDU), and examples of different land cover were manually outlined to train the computer to recognize a variety of sub-classes which were later aggregated into key cover types. The image analysis system employed by the ITE calculated the statistics for reflectances associated with each cover type, and extrapolated this knowledge to allocate each 25 m^2 cell to the most likely cover type based on this value. Digital masks of maritime, urban and upland areas were used to improve the final classification. The data were supplied by the ITE with 25 distinct classes of land cover (ITE, 1993) which were then aggregated into 15 simpler classes.

Primary Vector Maps and Coverages

The boundary, character zones and mineral activity coverages were captured in vector format from the Thames Chase Community Forest Plan. The Agricultural Land Classification coverage was captured from the MAFF map outlining the regions of agricultural land classifications. The major roads, rivers and railways were all captured from the Ordnance Survey 1:50 000 map of the area. The ARCEDIT module of PC Arc Info was used to digitize the coverages. The base map was derived from the Ordnance Survey 1:50 000 Landranger Series. Attributes were added using the Tables module of Arc Info.

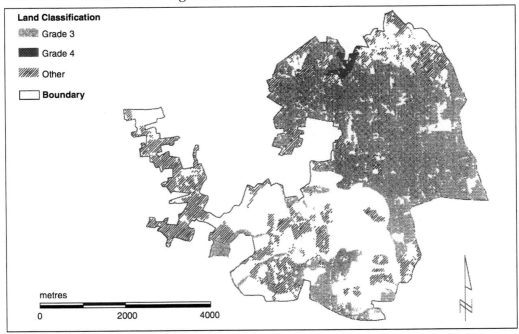

Figure 1. Implementation areas using grants criteria, showing agricultural land classification

Secondary Vector Coverages

To enable more sophisticated analysis of the datasets, composite or secondary vector coverages were produced. The first stage of this process was to create a vector coverage from the raster Land Cover image. This was achieved by importing the data into Arc Info using the GRIDPOLY module to produce a vector polygon coverage of the Land Cover data. The Thames Chase Community Forest Boundary, Mineral Activity and Agricultural Land Classification coverages were combined to produce a composite image which facilitates complex queries. Figure 1 shows the selection of areas which satisfy the conditions of being Grade 3 agricultural land or below, not already woodland, and within 8 km of an urban area.

The other important secondary vector coverage was created as a two stage process. First, the road and rail coverages were combined and a 30 m buffer polygon was generated around them. This coverage was then combined with Agricultural Land Classification data to produce a composite coverage. This allowed interrogation of the database to show areas of land within 30 m of road and railways on low grade agricultural land.

CONCLUSIONS

The amalgamation of data relating to land cover and agricultural land classification allows the identification of a priority model of Thames Chase implementation based on policy objectives. Considering the predominance of private land ownership structures within the project area, grant aid incentives are regarded as the primary instruments for converting policy into practice and thereby ensuring beneficial change. During an ethos of agricultural decline and restructure in an industry lacking firm traditions of farm:forest integration, projected planting goals have proved difficult to realize. However, forestry expansion on agricultural land remains a cornerstone of the Community Forest initiative, and improved grant packages have recently been introduced in an attempt to address this priority.

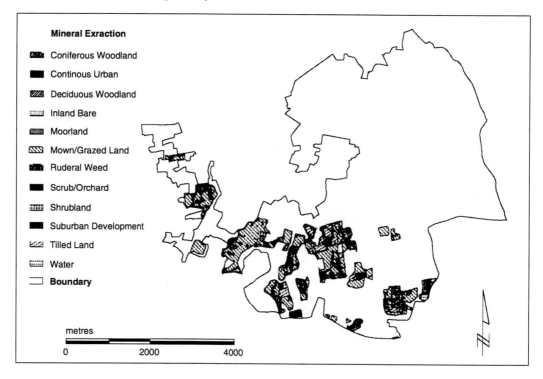

Figure 2. Land cover of sites of former mineral extraction with communication buffers

Using a model which prioritizes this approach as a focus for initial implementation, the northern part of the forest area, particularly the Brentwood Hills and the Plain of Thurrock character zones, has been identified for development. This would appear to suggest a conflict between the demands of policy implementation and the ultimate aim of promoting regeneration of the overall area. Regenerative efforts aim to improve local environments to stimulate investment and encourage visitors. The southern section of the forest, notably the Rainham and Ockendon character zone, suffers a range of difficulties associated with mineral extraction and as a result, experiences significant image related problems. In terms of implementation using regenerative criteria, enhancement of image is seen as a priority (Figure 2).

Much of the regeneration priority area is excluded from the policy objective model. This is partly due to the fact that rich mineral deposits often coincide with high quality agricultural land, and these areas are protected by the need to prevent irreversible development during a period of uncertainty within the farming industry. The presence of hope values and land speculation tend to exacerbate such limitations. Further areas of importance to the consideration of image improvement relate to plantings alongside transport corridors and in areas abutting urban and suburban building development.

The two models discussed in this paper represent different priorities for initial development of the Thames Chase area. The variance between selected criteria indicates a spatial division dependent upon the ranking of individual objectives. Land use conflicts can be widespread, and development strategies need to recognize a multiplicity of economic, social and environmental factors consistent with the principles of sustainable development. Limited focus on policy priority, as indicated in this paper, tends to reduce the effectiveness of initial implementation practices and therefore limits regenerative processes. An extension of this research to include social interactions is considered important in maximizing the availability of information for decision makers involved in promoting a holistic approach towards developing the Community Forest concept.

REFERENCES

Eastman, J., Kyem, P., Toledano, J. and Weigen, J. (1993) Explorations in Geographic Information Systems technology. In: *GIS and Decision Making*. Geneva: UNITAR.

Essex County Council, Brentwood District Council, Thurrock Borough Council, London Borough of Barking and Dagenham, London Borough of Havering. (1994) Thames Chase Plan.

ESRI (1993) *Understanding GIS*. Redlands, California: Environmental Systems Research Institute.

Evans, S. and Davis, D. (1993) A review of Community Forest Policy and the constraints on its implementation. *Environmental Policy and Practice*, 2(4): 399-411.

Forestry Commission (1995) *Woodland Grant Scheme Applicants Pack*. Farnham, UK: Forestry Commission.

Institute of Terrestrial Ecology (1993) Class Description Land Cover Map of Great Britain. Monkswood, UK: Natural Environment Research Council.

Moffat, A. and McNeil, J. (1994) Reclaiming disturbed land for forestry. *Forestry Commission Bulletin 110*. Edinburgh: Forestry Commission.

Geographic Information Systems for Protected Area Zonation at Garamba National Park, Zaire

Emmanuel de Merode[1], Monungu Likango[2] and Kes Hillman Smith[3]

[1]Department of Anthropology, University College, London, UK.
[2]Institut Zaïrois pour la Conservation de la Nature, Zaire.
[3]Garamba National Park Project, Zaire.

ABSTRACT

The Garamba ecosystem is of considerable value to African conservation because of its unique species. However, the socio-political context of the region makes conservation management extremely complex. This paper discusses the use of a simple geographic information system (GIS) as a decision support tool for the zonation of the National Park and its surrounding reserves. The products of this exercise are designed to serve the wide spectrum of decision makers in such a way that their comments and criticisms can be used to develop a better understanding of the ecosystem.

INTRODUCTION

Garamba National Park is situated in northeastern Zaire on the border with Sudan. Particular importance has been attached to this area because it is home to the last known wild population of the northern white rhino. This, together with the unique nature of the ecosystem, led to its classification as a UNESCO World Heritage Site in 1983, but the isolation and socio-political context of the region presents complex problems for protected area management.

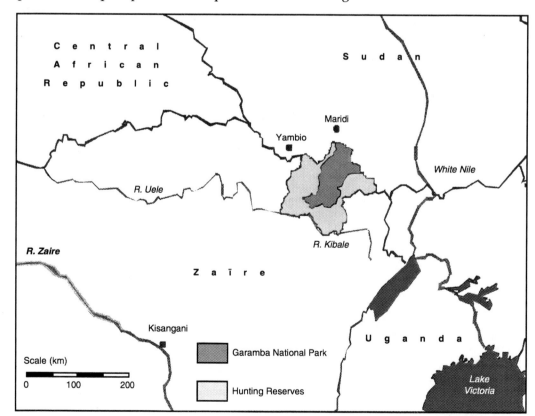

Figure 1. Study area

For wildlife management to meet a wide variety of conservation needs, it must be provided with accurate and appropriate information on ecological and socio-

120

economic developments in the area. In 1984, the Garamba National Park Research and Monitoring Programme was set up to collect and collate this information. Much of the data collected under the programme were spatially referenced, but while in extensive tabular form, they were sometimes difficult to interpret by management decision makers. In April 1994, a GIS was adopted as a means of analysing and presenting large amounts of information in an intuitively logical way, standardizing data collection procedures, and enhancing existing analytical procedures.

Recent efforts to develop a management plan for the ecosystem have highlighted the need for multiple management regimes, each designed according to the local ecological and social characteristics of a stochastic environment. A reliable blueprint for the zonation of protected areas has not been drawn, although various attempts have been made (IUCN, 1994). The management is acutely aware of the need to develop a framework which addresses the cultural, institutional, political and economic needs of the area while securing the overall objective for the conservation programme of maintaining the integrity of the ecosystem (Garamba National Park Project, 1995).

This paper will outline the ways in which various monitoring and research results were integrated to form a sound basis for the zonation of the National Park and reserves into management units, ranging from areas of strict conservation to areas for the sustainable utilization of natural resources. The work represents a first stage in the definition of management zones. Its outputs form a framework to be discussed and modified through the combined expertise of the National Park management and consultants from the local communities representing a cross-section of those groups.

BACKGROUND

Ecology

The Garamba ecosystem falls within the Sudano-Guinean biome between latitudes 3° and 5° North and 28° and 30° West. The area has one of the highest large mammal biomasses in Africa (Hillman Smith, 1989), most of which is concentrated in the National Park (4900 km^2). In addition to the 29 rhinos (Hillman Smith *et al.*, 1995), the Park has an endemic population of northern savanna giraffes (*Giraffa camelopardalis congoensis*), and the population of over 11 000 elephant (*Loxodonta africana*) represents the highest concentration in Zaïre. There is a stark contrast between the vegetation of the Park and the reserves. The southern two-thirds of the Park consist largely of long grass savanna dominated by *Loudetia arundinacea* and *Hypparrhenia* sp. Further north there is an increasing gradient of tree/bush savanna and woodland with dense gallery forest. The reserves bordering the Park have a contrasting vegetation community structure, composed largely of woodland and dense to medium tree/bush savanna, which includes species such as *Combretum collinum* and *Bauhinia thoningii*.

Socio-Economic Context

The Park is managed under a 'total protection' regime which excludes any human habitation or economic activity. By contrast, the three reserves, known as 'domaines de chasse', were gazetted to facilitate the sustainable management of the natural resources in the protected area for the benefit of local communities. The residents in and around the reserves can be broadly divided into three socio-economic groups. The first are resident agriculturalists who subsist largely from shifting agriculture with cassava (*Manihot* sp.) as the staple. Secondly, the Second Civil War in Sudan has had considerable social and demographic repercussions in this border region, with the arrival of over 90 000 Sudanese refugees in 1991. The majority have either taken up residence in settlements on the periphery of the reserves administered by the United Nations High Commissioner for Refugees and the local Catholic Diocese, or have 'self settled' within the reserves. Lastly, the gold deposits in the reserves have attracted an important gold mining industry in the south. These activities fall within the critically important Zaïrian informal economy. The exploitation of natural resources, particularly bushmeat (Asibey, 1986), from the protected area represents a survival strategy adopted by the communities living in one of the most economically marginalized regions of Africa.

Administration

The Park's administration falls under the authority of the Institut Zaïrois pour la Conservation de la Nature (IZCN), and collaborative support is provided by the Garamba National Park Project funded by the World Wide Fund for Nature, the Frankfurt Zoological Society, and several other non-governmental organizations. IZCN has overall responsibility for the running of the Park and the surrounding reserves, including law enforcement, infrastructural development, and the development of the reserves. However, work in the reserves has not been undertaken since colonial days, primarily due to a lack of resources. The project provides logistical and technical support for IZCN staff.

CONFLICTS

Cross Border Conflicts

Many of the protected area's management problems can be attributed to the high level of political instability in Southern Sudan (Suliman, 1992). The current Civil War in Sudan has been associated with a dramatic expansion in the level of organized poaching in the Park (Mesi, personal communication). This has been compounded by an increase in the availability of automatic weapons in the region since the fall of the major southern Sudanese towns of Yambio and Maridi in 1991. As a result, three partially supervised battalions of Zaïrian infantry have been stationed in the region. Poaching activities are characterized by the movement of large, highly organized and motivated bands which often out-number, and are better equipped than, the IZCN patrols. The distribution of 'accrochages' or shooting incidents between guards and poaching groups for 1993 is shown in Figure 2.

Land Use

The history of the Park is characterized by local resentment caused by conflict over access to resources. This dates back to the expropriation and resettlement of those populations formerly resident in the Park. Resentment and conflict is a characteristic of national parks throughout Africa where the interests of the resident communities have not been taken into consideration during the formulation of protected area systems (Western, 1993; Newmark *et al.*, 1993; Ghimire, 1994). The area has a relatively low human population density, and access to land is still organized on a communal rather than a freehold basis (Evans Pritchard, 1971; de Schlippé, 1986). Therefore, the conflicts over access to land for settlement and agriculture are less pronounced than those which result from the legal restrictions on the exploitation of wildlife (de Merode *et al.*, 1994). However, the successful wildlife conservation programme has led to a considerable increase in the abundance of large mammals and in certain areas, serious losses to agricultural productivity have resulted from animal crop raiding (Hillman Smith *et al.*, 1995). The development of gold mining activities has impacted on the conservation of the region both directly, in terms of the consequences of open cast mining and indirectly, through the increased demand for bushmeat and other resources from the protected area. The impact and distribution of these factors are not yet fully understood.

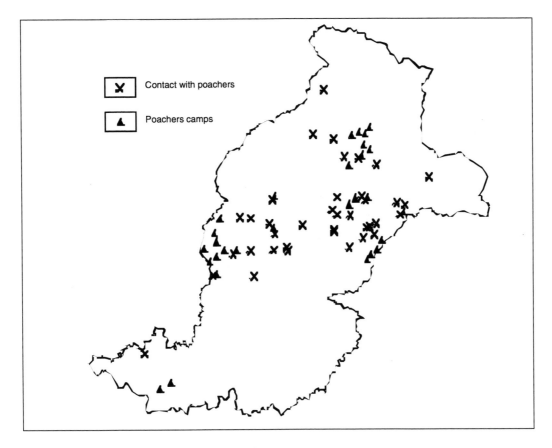

Figure 2. Reported illegal activities in the Park in 1993

PROTECTED AREA MANAGEMENT

Wildlife Protection

The scale and unpredictability of the illegal exploitation of wildlife within the National Park has meant that most of the Park's resources have been allocated to the control of poaching through armed patrols in the Park, and the provision of the logistical support and infrastructural developments needed to maintain these patrols. The objective of this strategy is to reduce the level of poaching and by so doing, enable wildlife populations to recover. Success may be measured by the 239% increase in the elephant population (from 3300 ± 509 in 1984 to 11 175 ± 3660 in 1995, $p = 0.05$) and the 106% increase in the rhino population (the population crashed from about 1500 in the 1960s to 15 in 1984 and has since increased to 29 in 1995) (Hillman Smith, 1989; Hillman Smith *et al.*, 1995).

Integrated Management

Although there has been a dramatic increase in the populations of most large mammal species between 1984 and 1995, experience in Garamba and elsewhere has shown that wildlife population are likely to crash in the absence of continued external donor support (Caughley, 1994). It is now accepted that a 'fortress' approach to conservation will not provide a long-term solution to the maintenance of a protected area in Africa (Adams and McShane, 1992; Barbier *et al.*, 1990) for two reasons. Although the legislation affecting national parks is drawn up at a national level (IUCN, 1994), a democratic process is expected to take effect eventually at the local government level. Unless the conservation activities are seen to provide tangible benefits to the resident communities, economic practices not necessarily suited to the sustainable exploitation of resources will predominate. Secondly, it is accepted that human communities are an integral part of the ecosystem, and unless their needs are taken into account, conservation initiatives will not be viable. Local communities already play an active role in resource management, but it is essential that they are recognized by the formal conservation management. Close collaboration between the Park management and a cross-section of community members is an appropriate and economically viable approach for ensuring that natural resources are rationally exploited, regulations observed, and the benefits of conservation properly communicated to the local communities.

PROTECTED AREA ZONATION

Integrated protected area management demands that a consensus be established for optimal land use policy. To achieve this, all parties are required to state their intended land use practices. This protracted process can be facilitated by a decision support tool which displays the distribution of resources and other factors pertinent to conservation. GIS technology has been used to integrate a variety of features which need to be incorporated into the development of land use policy. These include indicators of ecological value and human presence in combination with the distribution of other factors pertinent to conservation.

DATA SOURCES

Faunal Distributions Over the Entire Ecosystem
The primary source of data is the regular and systematic aerial sampling over the Park and reserves. Regular transects at 5 km intervals are flown at low altitude. Observers count and record observations within carefully calibrated strip widths on either side of the aircraft. The spatial precision of the recordings was enhanced by the use of a global positioning system (GPS), and a fixed elevation was maintained using a radar altimeter. In order to reduce the variability of the results, the study area was stratified, and standard statistical techniques were used to obtain estimates of the abundance of large mammal species and the number of huts in the reserves (Norton Griffiths, 1978). Data were exported to a GIS (ARC/INFO) in order to examine and analyse the results.

This technique does not, however, provide adequate results for areas with a high tree canopy, as in the reserves. These areas were surveyed over an 8 month period using line transects based on distance sampling techniques (Dawson and Decker, 1992). Transects 5 km apart were walked by a team of researchers who recorded mammal observations and signs of their presence (faeces, spoor and vegetation damage) (Nicolas and Ndey, 1994). This produced very precise, low intensity data which were generalized for the whole area using a weighted distance interpolation routine (Eastman, 1993).

Rhino Observations
The rhino population, which is the main focus of the research and monitoring programme, has been intensively monitored since 1984. A counting technique is used, based on individual recognition, and positions are recorded to within 1 km from the ground or from an aircraft.

Distribution of Illegal Activities in the Park
A survey technique for recording observations made by guards on patrol in the Park has been used since 1989 (Bell, 1984). Data are included on all encounters with poachers and any indication of their presence such as disused camps, poached carcasses and gunshots. Data entry sheets include field maps, and the dense network of rivers and streams in the Park, together with the pronounced local knowledge of the guards, ensures a relatively accurate positioning of observations.

Human Population Distribution

Currently, the only information on the distribution of the human population in the reserves is derived from the aerial hut count. A ground truthing exercise was carried out in the communities to determine the average number of people per hut. No reliable formal demographic data exist for this area.

Crop Damage

Figure 3 shows the results of a modelling exercise to identify areas of high elephant crop damage. The potential for crop damage was inferred from the combined occurrence of concentrated human settlement and high levels of elephant use of natural vegetation in the area. Parameters were based on a study of

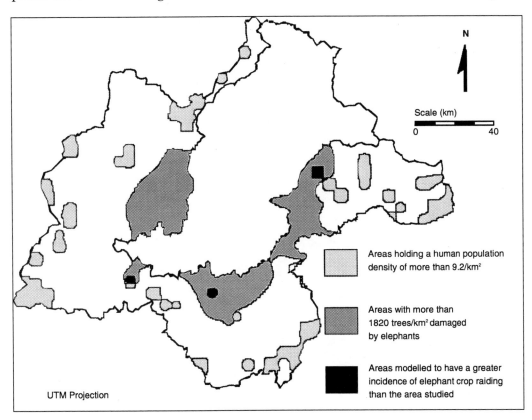

Figure 3. Modelling elephant crop damage

an area known to experience high levels of elephant crop damage. A programme to develop possible means of reducing the impact of elephants and other mammals is currently underway (Hillman Smith *et al.*, 1995).

RESULTS

Preliminary Zonation

Figure 4 shows the above data integrated into a single map and reflects our current understanding of the processes taking place in the ecosystem. Poaching is concentrated in the northern half of the Park, close to the border with Sudan, and is largely excluded from the more intensively monitored rhino sector in the south (depicted by an outer convex polygon joining the most peripheral rhino observations, thus suggesting a close approximation of the rhino home and extended range). The elephant population is also concentrated in the south. In the reserve, elephants are used as a keystone species to represent areas of high conservation value. Elephant natural vegetation damage was used as the most effective means of inferring their presence in the densely vegetated habitat.

Human population distribution is shown in the reserves, along with known refugee settlements and those areas known to be exploited for gold.

Figure 5 represents a preliminary zonation based on these data. The management of the Park still focuses on the need to control poaching. An intensively monitored rhino sector is contained within the central south area. This area is modified according to changes in the ranging behaviour of the rhino population. A central north area covered by two northern sector patrols acts as a buffer to prevent high levels of poaching spreading into the rhino sector. To the north of this, a peripheral area has been effectively abandoned as far as the patrolling effort is concerned, because of the excessive insecurity.

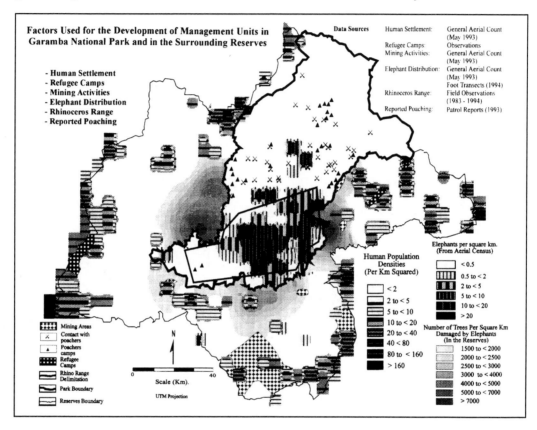

Figure 4. Factors used to define management zones

The zonation in the reserves represents the early stages of an integrated conservation development project. The area has been prioritized into areas of high conservation value and areas where developmental extension activities may take place. These delimitations are defined by easily identified landscape features which can be discussed more fully. Data on the spatial distribution of traditional political authority have been compiled to facilitate the refinement of this zonation through consultation with community representatives.

Consensus Building
Satisfactory zonation exercises potentially rely on vast amounts of accurate information. To some extent, this has been collected using various formal quantitative survey techniques. These techniques can be extremely intensive in terms of time and expense. However, they do provide a relatively objective baseline from which to work. Increasingly, this approach is being replaced by more qualitative, participatory forms of information gathering (FAO, 1989). These rely heavily on indigenous technical knowledge which is based on the reasonable assumption that local residents will be better informed about their

environment than outside researchers. Participatory management is a new approach which is expected to be implemented during the project's next phase. The zonation exercise at Garamba attempts to integrate the two approaches to obtain results which can be justified in a reasonably objective manner and which involve the knowledge of community representatives in the decision process. GIS provides an interface between the two approaches by presenting an intuitively logical display of quantitative results. These can be discussed, questioned and modified by all those involved in the decision process. This iterative process is still in its early stages and should continue to be modified as a response to the dialogue between Park authorities and community representatives. This is expected to take place through existing projects involving workshops and extensive participatory research with the communities.

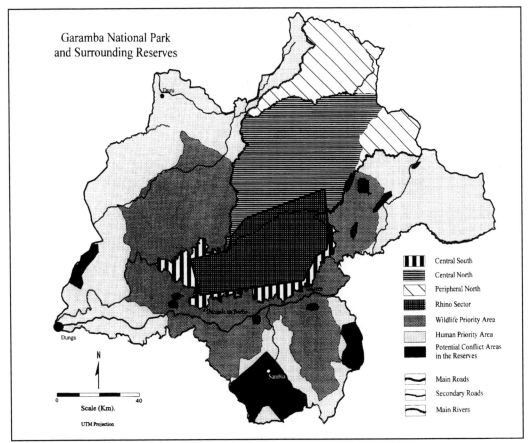

Figure 5. Management zones

DISCUSSION

This work demonstrates the use of spatial techniques to produce an interface between a research body and the current and future decision makers in the organization of a protected area. It is an attempt to make the scientific perspective on the distribution of resources more accessible to a wider audience, and thus to ensure significant participation in the decision process.

Community conservation, written in the currently fashionable language of aid organizations and academics, makes certain unrealistic assumptions. The enduring nature of the conflict between people and the protected areas suggests that there may never be full agreement between parties representing development and the environment. This is exacerbated by the political instability of the region resulting largely from the availability of automatic weapons; this leads to unequal access to natural resources and excludes the more vulnerable groups. As a result, wildlife consumption mostly benefits those who control this means of production, i.e., individuals who are not always concerned with the sustainability of the resource. Resource exploitation in the Park is currently under the control of those minorities with access to automatic weapons and their formal participation in the decision process is unlikely to be agreed upon by the National Park authorities. On the other hand, the surrounding reserves potentially provide a body of experts with a vested interest in the success of resource management.

CONCLUSION

This paper has discussed the use of a low-cost, relatively simple GIS for the organization of a framework for defining optimal land use zones in a protected area. A wide variety of survey data was used to produce an intuitively logical display of the factors and processes affecting the ecosystem. This was designed as a decision support tool for a wide cross-section of decision makers, all of whom are essential for effective protected management.

In conclusion, these results highlight the fact that the current level of understanding is insufficient to design an integrated land use policy for the protected area. This demands an effort on the part of the National Park management to involve local residents, not through passive participation designed to attract funding, but as experts taking part in an interactive community conservation programme.

ACKNOWLEDGEMENTS

The authors would like to thank the various institutions and individuals who have supported this work at Garamba: The Institut Zaïrois pour la Conservation de la Nature (IZCN); World Wildlife Fund for Nature (WWF); The Global Resource Information Database of the United Nations Environment Programme (UNEP/GRID). This paper was edited by Joanne Abbot, Katherine Homewood and two anonymous referees. In particular, we would like to thank the IZCN and project personnel, working under conditions of considerable hardship at Garamba, for their continued support

REFERENCES

Adams, J.S. and McShane, T.O. (1992) *The Myth of Wild Africa*. New York: W.W. Norton.

Asibey, E.O.A. (1986) *Wildlife and Food Security*. Paper prepared for the Forestry Department, FAO, Rome.

Barbier, E., Burgess, J., Swanson, T. and Pearce, D. (1990) *Elephants, Economics and Ivory*. London: Earthscan Publications Ltd.

Bell, R.H.V. (1984) Monitoring of illegal activities and law enforcement in African conservation areas. In: *Conservation and Management of Protected Areas. Proceedings of the U.S. Peace Corps Conference, Kasungu National Park, Malawi, 1983*.

Caughley, G. (1994) Directions in conservation biology. *Journal of Animal Ecology*, **63**: 215-244.

Dawson, S. and Dekker, A.J.F.M. (1992) *Counting Asian Elephants in Forests: a Techniques Manual*. Bangkok: FAO Regional Office for Asia and the Pacific.

Eastman, J.R. (1993) IDRISI: *A Grid Based Geographic Analysis System: Version 4.1*. Worcester, Masachusetts: Clark University, Graduate School of Geography.

Evans Pritchard, E.E. (1971) *The Azande: History and Political Institutions*. Oxford: Clarendon Press.

FAO (1989) *Community Forestry: Participatory Assessment, Monitoring and Evaluation*. Rome: FAO.

Garamba National Park Project (1995) *Draft framework document for the development of a management plan for Garamba National Park, Zaïre*. GNPP Internal Document.

Ghimire, K.B. (1994) Parks and people: livelihood issues in national parks management in Thailand and Madagascar. *Development and Change*, **25**: 195-225.

Hillman Smith, K. (1989) *Ecosystem resource inventory, Garamba National Park*. Internal Document, IUCN/WWF/FZS/IZCN.

Hillman Smith, K., Atalia, M., Likango, M., Smith, F., Ndey, A. and Panziama, G. (1995) *General aerial count 1995, and evaluation of the status and trends of the ecosystem*. WWF Garamba National Park Project.

IUCN (1994) *Guidelines for Protected Area Management Categories*. CNPPA with assistance from WCMC. Gland, Switzerland and Cambridge, UK: IUCN.

de Merode, E., Hillman Smith, K., Mbikongime, G., Obama, M., Panziama, G., To, A. and Kobode, E. (1994) *An assessment of attitudes towards rhino conservation at Garamba National Park and its surrounding Reserves*. Internal Report. Garamba National Park Project.

Newmark, W.D., Leonard, N.L., Sariko, H.I. and Gamassa, D.M. (1993) Conservation attitudes of local people living adjacent to five protected areas in Tanzania. *Biological Conservation*, **63**: 117-183.

Nicolas, A. and Ndey, A. (1994) *Mammal distributions in the reserves surrounding Garamba National Park, Zaire*. Internal Report, Garamba National Park Project.

Norton Griffiths, M. (1978) *Counting Animals*. AWF Handbook 1.

de Schlippé, P. (1986) *Ecoculture d'Afrique*. Collection Terres et Vie. Paris: L'Harmattan.

Soulé, M.E., Wilcox, B. and Holtby, C. (1979) Benign neglect: a model of faunal collapse in the game reserves of East Africa. *Biological Conservation*, **7**: 129-146.

Suliman, M. (1992) Civil war in Sudan: the impact of ecological degradation. *Environment and Conflicts Project, Occasional Paper no. 4*. Swiss Peace Foundation.

Western, D. (1993) *Conserving Savanna Ecosystems through Community Participation: the Amboseli Case Study*. Wildlife Conservation International.

Delegates

Surname	Initials	Title	e-mail	Address
ALDAKHEEL	Y Y	Mr	y.aldakheel@geography.salford.ac.uk	Telford Institute of Environmental Systems, University of Salford, Manchester, M5 4WT
ALLISON	S	Mr		158b, Hall Road, Norwich, NR1 2PP
AMABLE	G	Mr		
ASKEW	D	Mr	m128679@adas.co.uk	ADAS Leeds, Lawnswood, Otley Road, Leeds, LS16 5PY
BAKER	R H A	Dr	r.baker@csl.gov.uk	Central Science laboratory, MAFF, Hatching Green, Harpenden, Herts, AL5 2BD
BENNETT	J G	Mr	john.bennett@nri.org	Land Resources dept, NRI, Chatham Maritime, Chatham, Kent, ME4 4TB
BINGHAM	A	Mr	awb1001@cus.cam.ac.uk	Scott Polar Research Institute, University of Cambridge
BIRD	A C	Dr		Silsoe College, Cranfield University, Silsoe, Beds, MK45 4DT
BIRKETT	C	Dr	cmb@mssl.ucl.ac.uk	Mullard Space Science Lab, Holmbury St. Mary, Dorking, Surrey, RH5 6NT
BOAST	R	Dr		Division of Geography, School of Sciences, Staffordshire University, Leek Road, Stoke-on-Trent, ST3 2DF
BOLSDON	D	Mr	dbolsdon@ford.anglia.ac.uk	PHRG, Anglia Polytechnic University, Victoria Road, Chelmsford, CM1 1LL
BONIFACIO	R	Dr	swsbonif@reading.ac.uk	Dept of Meteorology, University of Reading, 2 Early Gate, Reading, RG6 2AU
BORDON	R W			49, Stormont Road, London, SW11 5EJ
BROWN	R	Dr	rob@rsac.demon.ac.uk	Remote Sensing Applications Consultants, Mansfield Park, Medstead, Alton, Hants, GU34 5PZ
BURGESS-ALLEN	P	Mr	pburgess@nrsc.co.uk	NRSC, Delta House, Southwood Crescent, Southwood, Farnborough, GU14 0NL
BUTTON	A P	Mr	lgxgapb@izn2.lass.nottingham.ac.uk	16 Robertson Close, Clifton-upon-Dunsmore, Rugby, Warks, CV23 0DJ
CALDWELL	A	Ms	100710.3722@compuserve.com	University College London, 6 Carshalton Way, Lower Earley, Reading, RG6 4EP
CAMPBELL	Ken			
CURR	R	Dr		Applied Sciences Faculty, Bath College of Higher Education, Newton Park, Bath, BA2 9BN
de MERODE	E	Mr		GIS Analyst, Garamba National Park Project, c/o AIM/MAF, P.O. Box 21285, Nairobi, Kenya
DEANE	G	Dr		Hunting Technical Services, Thames Field House, Boundary Way, Hemel Hempstead, HP2 7SR
EDWARDS	E	Ms	remote-sensing.HTS@city-scape.co.uk	
ERDAS (UK) Ltd				Dr Andy Wells, ERDAS (UK) Ltd, Telford House, Fulbourn, Cambridge, CB1 5HB
ERMAPPER				Dominic Cuthbert, Earth Resource Mapping Pty Ltd., Blenheim House, Crabtree Office Village, Eversley Way, Egham, Surrey, TW20 8RY
EVANS	S	Mr	for3187m@uel.ac.uk	Research Room E204, Anglia Polytechnic University, Victoria Road, Chelmsford, CM1 1LL
FORBES	A	Dr		28 Rutland Ct, Denmark Hill, London, SE5 8EB
GARRETT	A	Mr	andy.garrett@adas.co.uk	ADAS, Govt. Buildings, Lawnswood, Otley Road, Leeds, LS16 5PY
GITAS	I	Ms	ig10001@cus.cam.ac.uk	Dept of Geography, Downing Place, Cambridge, CB2 3EN
GREEN	E	Dr	e.r.green@ncl.ac.uk	Dept of Marine Science and Coastal Management, University of Newcastle, Newcastle upon Tyne, NE1 7RU
HAINES	I	Dr		ODA, 94, Victoria Street, London, SW1E 5JL
HAY	S	Mr	simon.hay@zoo.ox.ac.uk	TALA Research Group, Dept. of Zoology, South Parks Road, Oxford, OX1 3PS

Surname	Initials	Title	e-mail	Address
HUGHES	KJ	Dr	k.hughes@roehampton.ac.uk	Roehampton Institute, London, SW19 5NN
IDRISI			j.cheesman@mmu.ac.uk	Ms Jo Cheesman, IDRISI Resource Centre, Env & Geog Sciences Dept, Manchester Metropolitan University, Chester St, Manchester, M1 5GD
IRVING	A	Mr		University of Nottingham, 63, Mottram Road, Chilwell, Nottingham
JAMES	P	Mr	pcj@sea.co.uk	Systems Engineering & Assessment Ltd., Beckington Castle, PO Box 800, Bath, BA3 6TB
JARVIS	A	Ms	chj@geo.ed.ac.uk.	20 St Peters Place, Edinburgh, EH3 9PQ
JOHN WILEY				Dr. Iain Stevenson, John Wiley & Sons Ltd, Baffins Lane, Chichester, West Sussex, PO19 1UD
KING	R B	Dr	koh@bathhe.ac.uk	NRI, Chatham Maritime, Chatham Kent, ME4 4TB
KOH	A	Mr		RSGIS Unit, Bath College of Higher Education, Newton Park, Bath, BA2 3BN
LAW	J	Dr	j.law@pvs.aff.gov.uk	NIAB, Huntingdon Road, Cambridge, CB3 0LE
LEWCOCK	C	Mr	chris.lewcock@nri.org	NRI, Chatham Maritime, Chatham, Kent, ME4 4TB
MEADEN	G J	D	g.j.mearden@canterbury.ac.uk	Canterbury Christ Church College, North Holmes Road, Canterbury, Kent, CT1 1QU
MILES	A			
MITCHELL	C W	Dr	alex1@mdx.ac.uk	ISMARSC Ltd, 57 Knox Green, Binfield, Bracknell, Berks, RG12 5NZ
MOON	A	Mr	p.j.mumbt@sheffield.ac.uk	GIS Laboratory, Middlesex University, Queensway, Enfield, EN3 4SF
MUMBY	P	Mr	steve.newby@vega.co.uk	Department of Geography, University of Sheffield, Winter Street, Sheffield. S10 2TN
NEWBY	S	M		Vega Group, Shire Park. Welwyn Garden City, Herts, AL7 1TW
NIGEL PRESS ASSOCIATES Ltd				Renalt Capes, Nigel Press Associates Ltd, Edenbridge, Kent, TN8 6HS
PACKER	M J	Mr	epatrick@geog.ucl.ac.uk	15 York Terrace East, Flat 1a, London, NW1 4PT
PATRICK	E	Mr	gperoni@geog.ucl.ac.uk	10, Clapham Ct, Kings Avenue, London, SW4 8DU
PERONI	G	Mr		GIU, English Nature, Northminster House, Peterborough, Cambs, PE1 1UA
POLY	M	Mr		Silsoe College, Cranfield University, Silsoe, Beds, MK45 4DT
PRATT	N D	Mr	dprodger@ordsvy.govt.uk	Ordnance Survey International, Romsey Road, Southampton, SO16 4GU
PRODGER	D	Mr		Land Resources Monitoring and Remote Sensing, Silsoe College, Cranfield University,
SANNIER	C	Mr		Silsoe, Beds, MK45 4DT
SCHNEIDER	H	Dr	itfmp@server.indo.net.id	Indonesia Tropical Forest Management Programme, c/o LTS International, 10 Woodhall Millbrae, Edinburgh, EH14 5BJ
SHEN	J	Mr		c/o Faculty Office, Dartford Campus, University of Greenwich, Dartford, Kent.
STRAWBRIDGE	F	Dr		RSGIS unit, Applied Sciences Faculty, Bath College of Higher Education, Newton Park, Bath, BA2 9BN
STUDDARD	M	Mr	matthews@eos.co.uk	EOS Ltd, Broadmede, Farnham Business Park, Farnham, GU9 8QL
SWEET	J	Mr		RSS, 8 Boyne House, 55 Blackwater Road, Eastbourne, BN20 7DL
TADROSS	M	Mr	mat1002@cus.cam.ac.uk	Scott Polar Research Inst, University of Cambridge, Lensfield Road, Cambridge, CB2 1ER
TAYLOR	J	Dr	j.c.taylor@cranfield.ac.uk	Professor of Land Resource Monitoring and Remote Sensing, Silsoe College, Cranfield University, Silsoe, Beds, MK45 4DT

Surname	Initials	Title	e-mail	Address
TEEUW	R	Dr	r.m.teeuw@herts.ac.uk	Environmental Sciences, University of Hertfordshire, College Lane, Hatfield, Herts, AL10 9AB
THOMPSON	P			NRI, Chatham Maritime, Chatham, Kent, ME4 4TB
TURNER	S	Mr	simon_turner@adas.co.uk	ADAS, Woodthorne, Wolverhampton, WV6 8TQ
USHER	E	Mr		Environmental Sciences, University of Hertfordshire, College Lane, Hatfield, Herts, AL10 3AB
VIRGO	K	M		WS Atkins, Wellbrook Ct, Girton, Cambridge, CB3 0NA
WADSWORTH	R	Dr	raw@nmt.ac.uk	Environmental Information Centre, Monks Wood Institute of Terrestrial Ecology
WEIR	M	Dr	weir@itc.nl	ITC, 350 Noulevard 1945, PO Box 6, 7500 AA Enschede, The Netherlands
WICKETT	M	Mr	100723.3132@compuserve.com	Gurney Consultants, Gurney Electronics Ltd., 12 Albert Street, Cambridge, CB4 3BE
WOOSTER	M	Mr	m.j.wooster@open.ac.uk	Earth Science Department, Open University, Milton Keynes
WU	TIAN	Mr		c/o Faculty Office, Dartford Campus, University of Greenwich, Dartford, Kent

SPONSORS

Company	Contact	Address
ERDAS (UK) Ltd	Dr Andy Wells	ERDAS (UK) Ltd., Telford House, Fulbourn, Cambridge, CB1 5HB
ERMAPPER	Dominic Cuthbert	Earth Resource Mapping Pty. Ltd., Blenheim House, Crabtree Office Village, Eversley Way, Egham, Surrey, TW20 8RY
IDRISI Resource Centre.	Ms Jo Cheesman j.cheesman@mmu.ac.uk	IDRISI Resource Centre, Env & Geog Sciences Dept, Manchester Metropolitan University, Chester St. Manchester, M1 5GD
IS Ltd,		Atlas House, Atlas Business Centre, Manchester, M22 5HF
JOHN WILEY & SONS	Dr. Iain Stevenson	John Wiley & Sons Ltd, Baffins Lane, Chichester, West Sussex, PO19 1UDT
NIGEL PRESS ASSOCIATES LTD	Renalt Capes	Nigel Press Associates Ltd., Edenbridge, Kent, TN8 6HS
OVERSEAS DEVELOPMENT ASSOCIATION	Dr. Ian Haines	ODA, 94 Victoria Street, London, SW1E 5JL
REMOTE SENSING SOCIETY	Dr C.W.Mitchell	The Remote Sensing Society, Department of Geography, University of Nottingham, NG7 2RD
TAYLOR & FRANCIS Ltd,	Karen Rooney	Taylor & Francis Ltd, Rankine Road, Basingstoke, Hants, RG24 8PR

NRI AND STAFF ORGANIZERS

Baxter	Alistair	UoG	UoG Welcome Address
Brown	Pat	UoG	Technical Support
Charapuka	Tariro	UoG	Registration
Cocks	Fiona	UoG	UoG Course Representative, Poster Paper Co-ordinator
Couzens	John	UoG	Registration
Downey	Ian	NRI	Afternoon Session Chair and Panel Discussion Co-ordinator
Foxwell	Hilary	UoG	UoG Publicity, Display Stands
Grist	Sally	UoG	Registration
Hayward	Richard	UoG	Technical Support
Howett	John	UoG	Technical Support
Higgs	Martin	UoG	Poster Display
Howe	Valerie	NRI	NRI Publications Representative
Kiteley	Barry	UoG	Poster Display
Lowry	Florence	UoG	UoG Publicity, Display Stands
Mills	Alan	NRI	Sponsorship Co-ordinator, Sponsors Representative
Mitchell	Colin	RSS	RSS Welcome Address and RSS Representative
Pender	Judith	NRI	Panel Discussion Raporteur
Perovic	Natasha	UoG	Refreshments
Pole	Richard	UoG	Poster Display Team leader
Power	Clare	UoG	Morning Session Chair and Conference Organizer
Robert	Ridgeway	NRI	Panel Discussion Assistant Co-ordinator
Rosenberg	Jane	NRI	Keynote Speakers Representative
Rutter	John	NRI	NRI Representative
Sbandi	Franco	UoG	Poster Display, Refreshments
Schmid-McGibbon	Gesche	UoG	Panel Discussion Raporteur
Thompson	Peter	NRI	Keynote Session Chair, and NRI Welcome Address
Williams	Jim	NRI	Panel Discussion Assistant Co-ordinator
Wright	Michael	UoG	Poster Display
Yearbury	Gail	UoG	Registration